Rugby for Coach and Player

Rugby for Coach and Player

Don Rutherford

Arthur Barker Limited
5 Winsley Street London W1

SBN 213 00243 4

Printed in Great Britain by
Bristol Typesetting Company Limited, Bristol

Contents

Acknowledgements

Bob McEwen (Cambridge University and Scotland) for his advice and great knowledge of the game.
Stuart Emery for his artwork.
Miss Ellen Green for typing my manuscript.

Foreword

This excellent book, written by Mr Don Rutherford, is a personal effort to help the coach and the player of Rugby Football. It is a splendid contribution to the game and I hope will be widely read and discussed.

Mr Don Rutherford is a famous old England International full-back, a trained Physical Education teacher and the Technical Administrator to the Rugby Union responsible for schools and the training of coaches. He has shown great initiative in organising courses in many parts of the country, and I warmly commend his book to all who are interested in the game.

W. C. RAMSEY
President, Rugby Football Union
1970–1

An Introduction

1
The Theme

As a player one was on occasions reminded by those whose infectious enthusiasm had almost overcome them, ' to forget the ball and get on with the b . . . game '. Whilst hardly being a disciple of such a policy, if for no other reason than that it is a difficult game to play without the ball, one is constantly reminded that much is taken for granted in Rugby Union Football and that there has not been a great deal of textbook literature over the years.

One hopes that the beginner, either coach or player, the selector and the administrator, will find in this book something to broaden their interest, help to increase their knowledge, and more important, get things in perspective and the priorities right. For the more experienced then, some of this may be seen as old hat, but certainly not all of it and consequently, it is earnestly hoped, it may sufficiently stimulate even the very experienced coaches, players, selectors and administrators to see their rugby in a new light. If it does, then this book will have been well worthwhile.

At best Rugby Union Football is a free flowing game where fifteen athletic players combine together to produce an abundance of *spectacular* movement before a large and appreciative audience. At its worst it is fifteen half-fit individuals stumbling and bumbling through eighty minutes of hell, affording enjoyment neither to themselves nor to the handful of spectators present. Enjoyment has always been the corner-stone of rugby administrators' thinking since the game was founded some hundred-odd years ago.

This is vital to grasp immediately because unless changes

have been thought to be for the good of the players and their consequent enjoyment then change has not been welcomed. Time has proved this to be a good yardstick because the game continues to flourish and is ever growing in Europe, the Far East and America.

There have, of course, been many resistances in certain quarters to change in the actual preparation for and playing of the game. Happily, the last decade has seen the gradual erosion of the entrenched views and as people have seen that we can improve our knowledge and skill in art and science, without undue harm, then there is no conceivable reason why we should not similarly improve the knowledge and skill of our leisure pursuits.

Coaching in schools has always been accepted, but for some odd reason it has never been felt necessary to continue this education in the vast majority of British rugby clubs, that is until the last decade, and consequently any good work done at school level has been largely wasted or neglected thereafter and even a cursory glance at international results against Commonwealth teams since the turn of the century will show the folly of such negligence.

| | New Zealand (1905 onwards) | | | | | | South Africa (1903 onwards) | | | | | |
	P	W	L	D	F	A	P	W	L	D	F	A
England	8	1	7	0	52	104	6	1	4	1	20	40
Scotland	5	0	4	1	18	47	8	3	5	0	38	104
Ireland	5	0	5	0	17	58	8	1	6	1	48	124
Wales	8	3	5	0	47	110	7	0	6	1	15	61
British Isles	19	2	15	2	122	278	24	3	16	5	168	309

As I have previously indicated, in any textbook on rugby there must inevitably be a lot of material that is simple and obvious, albeit vitally necessary, but there is an onus on the thinking player and coach to use this material and manipulate it in such a way as to bring out the individual skills of each member of his team and at the same time formulate a team pattern or system of play that makes best use of the available material. Regrettably there has rarely been enough time given to thinking and even less to practising as a team.

In the British Isles the game has leant heavily on the idea that the sole purpose of the forwards was to get the ball, and the sole prerogative of the backs was to use it in an effort to score tries. Unhappily to corrupt Kipling's words ' the twain ne'er seem to have met!' Our Commonwealth cousins, whilst being the first to admit that ' forwards win matches ', have shown year in, year out, that when the forwards get the ball from scrum or line-out, this is just the beginning of their job and not the end. The two units, forwards and backs, must understand what the other is doing and the quicker this is achieved then the better they will play as a team.

We have so often forgotten that this is a fifteen-man team game; a point that I shall endeavour to stress time and time again.

In rugby we have to use our limbs, trunk and brain and whilst this must place tremendous demands on the individual, it does at least theoretically allow room for much improvisation. Even allowing for the fact that the ball has to be passed backwards in order to make progress forward our approach has been remarkably stereotyped.

One cannot help but feel that we have not used the available space as well as we might, maybe our deployment of players could be improved upon and certainly our brains are under-used on a Saturday afternoon. Now this might seem excessively hard criticism of those who turn out week in, week out, for the sheer fun of it.

But the question is ' How much better could they be and thus how much more they would enjoy their rugby '. If they thought more about it and practised more effectively, note, I did not say ' spent more time ' – then I cannot help but feel that their enjoyment would be immeasurably increased.

I should hasten to point out that there have been some wonderful club and international matches in the British Isles and some quite outstanding players, but improvements have tended to be spasmodic rather than sustained and this is probably due to our game lacking a basic depth of overall understanding.

Today's game is made up of twenty-seven laws and this in itself is interesting because originally there were virtually none. We are all familiar with the old adage that 'Laws were meant to be broken' and whenever the law makers have made changes or modifications to the Laws of the Game, lack of thought and/or a negative approach for most players and their teams has usually resulted in a further change or modification having to be made in due course.

A fairly recent example of this lack of thought was apparent when the 'Australian Dispensation Law', as it was called, was incorporated in the Laws for a trial period. The object of this law was to discourage kicking on the full into touch between the twenty-fives and to encourage running with the ball and for the most part it appears to have been immensely successful, but there were certainly many, full backs in particular, whose only answer was to run yards back into their twenty-five area in order to find a direct touch.

They had not anticipated the possibilities of the law, nor had their team mates who were invariably seen waiting, standing hands on hips, expecting the full back to give them a rest by kicking the ball into touch as under the previous law. They should, of course, have been moving back to take part in any counter-attack.

Other law changes of real importance have concerned the old time wing forwards, more accurately referred to as flank or loose forwards today, and the moment of time they could leave scrums and line-outs to terrorize opposition half-backs. Today's law giving ten yards breathing space from a line-out and keeping the loose forwards attached to scrums or behind the hindmost foot until the ball is out of the scrum seems eminently sensible. Let us hope that players and coaches will fully explore the possibilities for running and handling which these changes have presented.

There have been hundreds of minor changes in the laws over the years, all of which have endeavoured to add to the scope of the game. Admiral Sir Percy Royds said in his book *The History of the Laws of Rugby Football,* ' Laws may come and laws may go, but the game goes on forever '.

The significant point that players and now coaches should remember is just this, the game does go on forever and it is beholden on everyone to be positive in their approach, to note that law changes often bring with them a change in an individual's and possibly a team's role and that this is essentially a handling and running game, where quick wits count for so much.

If these points are noted then a truly exhilarating spectacle will follow and the British Isles, as the birthplace of the game, should be able to contribute as much in the future to the game as it obviously did at its inception.

We have plenty of natural talent which has rarely been organized or else has become despondent through lack of outlet valves to the top. Getting international recognition has been too chancy a business in the past and even when the opportunity has been presented, few have known how to cope with it. This has not been the individual's fault, but that of a system which has thrown together talented players without giving them adequate preparation for the task in hand.

We can do nothing but improve if we increase our understanding of the game, and correct coaching and the organization it implies can work wonders in this direction. There are a significant number of schools, clubs, and counties who are doing just this and their efforts should be a spur to the less active.

What follows should clear up a number of myths and point the way to more enjoyable rugby. To begin with we should all understand the correct meaning of the terms that we use in rugby.

10% of the problem. This point can be admirably illustrated by looking at the two words ' training ' and ' practice '.

The word ' training ', as far as club rugby has been concerned, has meant that on two evenings per week players arrived at their clubs and spent anything from 10 to 60 minutes cavorting up and down the pitch, performing the most weird and wonderful exercises in order to get themselves in reasonable shape for Saturday afternoon. This is an unrealistic and unnecessary waste of time, and one which does not endear itself to anyone other than the masochist.

Now why is it unrealistic and an unnecessary waste of time? Simply because on a Saturday afternoon you use a ball and are required to perform a great number of skills under extreme pressure. ' All right ', I can hear you saying, ' but we've got to be fit '. Granted, but in a recreational pastime – and this surely is what it is – you must use the time that you have allocated to match preparation in the most effective way possible.

Therefore, you would always use a ball and go through selected individual, unit and team skills under pressure in both your weekly PRACTICE sessions. You will now note that I have eliminated the word ' training '.

Now, do not misunderstand me, there is a place for physical training – there must be because the fitter you are the more chance you will have of displaying your skills, but ideally you would arrive at a practice session ' fit to practise ' and not arrive unfit and waste time by training. I realize that this attitude I am suggesting is laughable in relation to the vast majority of British rugby players or at least it was five years ago; but attitudes are changing and rugby is much faster today and the players are much fitter.

Many clubs have managed to make one of the two club evenings a practice session and the other a physical training session. This is a commendable step forward and I have no doubt in the not too distant future both club evenings

2
Understanding Rugby Terms

For a long time now we have heard people pontific
the virtue of us mastering the basics of rugby football
what do they mean? If they are talking about our abi
pass, run, kick and tackle, then they are referring to the
skills, which are unquestionably of very great importa

It should also be pointed out that basic skills are o
part of the skills that an individual player should pos
one must add to this, positional skills, to make the
dividual truly skilful. For example, how to shove i
scrum, how to hook, how to jump in a line-out, would
skills which only affect certain players and, therefore,
known as positional skills.

However, not all people limit the meaning of the te
'basics of rugby fotball' to individual skills (basic a
positional) – many are referring to other skills which a
basic to the game such as ruck, maul, line-out and scru
These are known as UNIT SKILLS and a blend of individu
and unit skills is likely to produce a clearer understan
ing of team play. Fifteen men playing together as a team
a skill all on its own. It means that fifteen individuals wi
have to understand the respective roles of each other an
be prepared to work and organize themselves so that eacl
knows what is on, and where it is on and which players wil
be carrying out the task.

If a mastery of the basics of rugby footbal is now to incorporate these three main skills, INDIVIDUAL, UNIT and
TEAM, then we are indeed all talking the same language and
have a clear objective in mind. Regrettably, however, this
is not the case and so often 90% of our effort is spent on

B

will be practice sessions with players arriving fit to practise, or, where travelling involves difficulty there could be one team practice session per week to which players are expected to come fit, being left to get fit in their own time and at their own convenience.

This one change in attitude, with the correct organization at club level, could revolutionize British rugby. In all of this, I have not mentioned school rugby, and quite deliberately, because the circumstances are different. Essentially school rugby provides a teaching and learning environment, whereas club rugby is ideally concerned with coaching and continued learning through playing experience. However, there is no doubt that it would help enormously if senior school boys were encouraged to think of going into club rugby after they had left school fit to practise. A pride in one's personal conditon is not a bad habit to acquire!

Further confusion or at least lack of clear thinking is evident when we talk about two aspects of forward play. One is simple and obvious and that concerns the words, loose scrum, which have now been superseded by the single word RUCK. A loose scrum inevitably ended up as a conglomeration of flying arms and legs and completely lacking in form. The selection of these two words may have been appropriate at the time because a ruck does closely resemble a scrum; unfortunately, it does not resemble a loose scrum. Exactly the opposite. Whether ruck is the appropriate word is open to doubt, but at least it is better than loose scrum, and should be used.

The other point of confusion concerns the terms ' second row ' and ' back row '. As practically every team packs down 3 : 4 : 1; it is obvious that there are four people in the second row and only one in the back. The two middle players of our second row are called LOCKS and this is important to grasp because as the word lock would suggest, they can and should be able to lock a scrum so that (a) it is tight, (b) it does not get pushed backwards (see chapter on

Forwards as Individuals). The words second row merely indicate any one of four people – the word lock tells us something about the duties of the two players in this position. A
useful distinction.

At the same time, it would help if rugby masters and team
secretaries wrote out forward positions in the correct order,
that is, from left to right, 1 Prop (loose head): 2 Hooker:
3 Prop (tight head): 6 Flanker: 4 Lock: 5 Lock:
7 Flanker: 8 No 8. It may seem a trifling point, but I think
not, because if we persist in writing them down as 3:2:3
scrum formation, namely: 1 Prop (loose head): 2 Hooker:
3 Prop (tight head): 4 Second row: 5 Second row: 6
Wing forward: 8 Lock; 7 Wing forward, players
will misguidedly be encouraged to carry out the role
of players in a 3:2:3 scrum which in the case of the
flankers and No 8 forward would be quite ineffective. As
the Laws of the Game stand at the moment, it is virtually
impossible for a flank forward to catch the opposition outside half from a scrum. Yet so many continue to attempt
this feat, which means leaning instead of pushing on a
scrum in an effort to flash away as soon as the ball is out.

If people think that a 3:4:1 scrum is a more effective
scrum, well then, for goodness' sake, let us use it properly,
that is, all seven or eight forwards pushing (you must in
part discount the push from the hooker on his own ball if
he strikes).

No wonder we struggle against New Zealand and South
African forwards when nine times out of ten, it is their eight
pushing against our six. It is hardly surprising that our forwards look lethargic long before the end of a match.

There are, of course, other rugby terms which for those
interested can be found in the Rugby Football Union's publications, *A Guide for Coaches* and *A Guide for Players*.
However, the ones that I have just outlined more often than
not present people with the most opportunity for making
mistakes. If the correct terminology could be used by every-

one then the phrase ' terminology breeds attitude ' would
have real significance.

The sort of attitude that rugby administrators are after
would involve players and coaches striving for perfection
through playing attacking rugby, where cheating was un-
heard of and the spirit of the game held equal place with
the laws of the game. These are not smug and wishful plati-
tudes, but very real needs in a hard bodily-contact team
game.

Begin by getting your terminology right and this will help
to breed the desired attitude.

3

Captain, Coach Relationship

The importance of the captain and the growing need for each team to have a coach is such that their respective roles and relationship should be assessed before looking at the actual contents of a game. Perhaps one might look upon these two individuals as having the respective roles of joint managers of a company. The company in this case being the playing affairs of a club. A school rugby captain and his rugby master will hardly be on the same footing, but their relationship should reflect that only *one* of them can play the game.

The great danger of any coach is that he should become too authoritarian and too detailed, the great danger of any captain is that he should feel he knows it all. No coach, let alone player, knows all that there is to know, and, therefore, captain and coach must use each other. A captain is not simply the man who decides which end to *attack*, his role is much more encompassing.

Because the position of the captain is an old and established one, let us look at some of the qualities he should possess. First and foremost, a personality which allows him to get the very best out of the other fourteen players. This will start on practice nights, but more important be reflected in the team's performance on the field.

Finding an outstanding captain is quite a problem, and many people would subscribe to the view that an outstanding captain would be picked by virtue of his leadership before the other fourteen players, even though his playing ability might be slightly below the desired standard. This may work at school and club level, but at county and international level you are taking quite a chance.

Once we get into the higher levels of the game, the fifteen players should be picked on the premise that they are the best fifteen individuals available at that moment of time. Your problem then, and it is a very real one, is to find a captain. It is too risky to play a person whose skills are not good enough. The team will suffer. To this, one should add that the captain, and the players on his team, should be able to read the game to such an extent that the captain can modify the tactics of the team as circumstances dictate.

Going back to one of my first points – all coaches must realize that they cannot play the game for their team. Their role is one of achieving a full acceptance of a framework to which the players' own ideas and flair can be harnessed. Once they step on to the pitch the players are all on their own, and if the captain and coach have done their job properly, they will have educated their players to such a pitch that if their original plans do not work, the players will not plod on like robots, but be sufficiently flexible to change their tactics within the overall framework. A few words about tactics at this point.

If you watch the All Blacks, the Springboks and the French, you would soon observe that, in spite of the fact that they are all playing rugby football, they have each evolved a different yet recognizable way of playing the game.

They each have their own pattern or system. There are many reasons why this has come about, different temperaments, different physiques, etc. Even so, within each of these various patterns or systems, modifications and change, that is tactics, have often to be made from match to match quickly and efficiently, according to the following considerations.

(a) *The strengths and weaknesses of your own players as well as those of the opposition.* As a general rule, you should know your own strengths and weaknesses before the match starts, and you may even know by reputation the strengths and weaknesses of your opponents. But, even if you do not, you must sum them up as soon after the kick-off as possible.

(b) *Weather and ground conditions*. If you start the match in brilliant sunshine, and after about twenty minutes you find yourself ankle deep in water, it is pretty obvious that your tactics will either have to be completely changed, or, at least, modified. If the wind is exceptionally strong, and in your favour, you can negate the advantage you have by over-kicking.

(c) *Injuries*. Injuries which cause team changes before a match and those which occur during the course of a game may completely disrupt your pattern or system. Your tactics would accordingly change or be modified. Opponents who lose a man through injury must have a weakness somewhere. You should spot it and turn it to your advantage. A note of warning. You can overplay on the opposition's weakness to such an extent that you miss orthodox opportunities to score. A balance is required.

(d) *Team understanding*. The greater or lesser the extent to which the players understand both the overall game and the organization of rucks, mauls, line-outs and scrums, and moves from short penalties, the more successful the team should be! For example, someone is promoted to a team and he is not fully conversant with the play of that team (this is poor club or school organization), then the end product will suffer. The astute captain will read the situation and change his tactics accordingly.

(e) *The state of the match*. In seven-a-side, you will probably recall seeing a captain who has elected not to take the kick at goal, particularly if it is wide out, so as to save time. Similarly in fifteen-a-side, a captain may decide to take a short penalty and go for five points rather than have the kick at goal for only three points. Again, if a penalty kick misses, the opponents have possession, with a short penalty they do not. The correct action by the captain can turn apparent defeat into victory, and by the same token, the incorrect action can have the reverse effect.

Generally speaking, to change your tactics on the field of play requires the ability to read the game. Some players are better than others at this facet of the game, but captain and coach should encourage players to know the reason why they are doing a particular action rather than being told to simply do it. The younger you are when this takes place, the better. An important point for schoolmaster coaches.

Moving to the coach at club level; he is in the position, by virtue of his playing experience, his knowledge of the laws, and his ability to communicate with and motivate people. Provided he has these qualities and is prepared to keep up-to-date with developments in the game, then he is the man best suited to organize and run a practice session.

A good captain and coach will get together before the season begins, have a definite aim in mind and plan how best their aim can be achieved. Their planning must be progressive which means that periodically they must take stock of what they have done and if necessary realign their aim accordingly.

No decent captain or coach would dream of turning up to a practice session without having prepared the contents of the session in detail. If schoolboys can spot the teacher who has not prepared his work, then club players are even more than likely to spot the coach who has not prepared his material. Once they see that you are organized and the sessions are progressive they will join in willingly. It's hard work, but rewarding.

Success through Simplicity-A Way of Thinking

4
The Method

It is very important to recognize that coaching is often seen, even now after many years of use, as being purely a mechanical skill wherein tactics are discussed *ad nauseam* and often without being related to the whole game. In fact, what is required at all levels is some very clear thinking at the strategical and team concepts level. People who have had some experience of team coaching will realize the significance of thinking conceptually, and not just technically.

The really effective coach should also expand his craft to embrace an understanding of the personality and performance of his players and how they interact. Without this understanding the coach's technical knowledge alone will be insufficient to get the very best out of each player.

There is much confusion because coaching is too often wrongly implemented through coaches' lack of insight into the priorities (the Key Factors of Chapter Five), but more in particular because they do not have a real overall view of the game and what they expect from it. Very few seem to know where they are going. They have not looked ahead and said, ' What do we want our rugby to be like in say, the mid-seventies?'

Because they have not projected their mind forward they have no model on which to work, which in turn is because they have never taken the trouble to sit down and work out the answer. They do not see beyond the next match or practice session.

It seems ironic, but people still say that words like philosophy and concepts are difficult to understand, yet these very same people will spend hours on detail, without having a real framework, thereby adding to, rather than reducing, the complexity and confusion surrounding the game and its improvement. Such people make it more difficult for themselves in the end, but of course simpler at the beginning. What they must realize is that the hard graft comes first and the details look after themselves – i.e. easily fall into a pattern.

It is vital to get down to the mental discipline and strenuous efforts needed for conceptual thought right at the outset, so as to obtain a sound framework. To achieve some early improvement by going direct to the detail is really a soft option and in the long run a disaster. Perhaps this is why New Zealand have been so successful over the years; they have a framework within which every individual player, school, club and province operates. They do not get bogged down with detail, but think simply, spend time only on the key factors and, consequently, they have developed an easily recognizable pattern of play that is both efficient and effective.

Not only have we failed to produce a recognizable pattern of play, but we have been ineffective (see results table, page 12) and very inefficient. Now I can hear certain people say ' But no New Zealander would talk this way, he would never mention the word " concepts "!' You are probably right, but whether the New Zealanders realize it themselves, they think this way. They seem to know where they are going and have done for some considerable time, consequently they are invariably one jump ahead.

To illustrate or reinforce this point have a look at figures 1(a) and 1(b).

You will see that 1(a) causes an anti-feeling against coaching and 1(b) produces a pro-feeling towards coaching in the long term, whereas the reverse is true in the short term.

If you accept this as being true then we must adopt

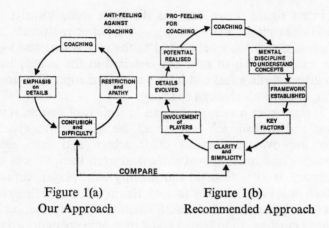

Figure 1(a)   Figure 1(b)
Our Approach   Recommended Approach

method (b) and have a framework from which to work. Therefore figure 2 ought to help everyone, players, captains, coaches and selectors alike, to understand the game as a whole and see where they are going at the outset.

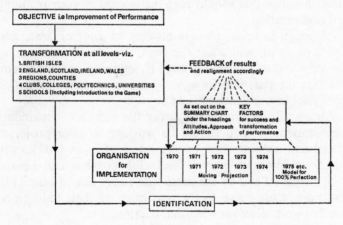

Figure 2

From figure 2 we can see the aims quite clearly; the individual player wishes to become a better performer, the team wishes to play better, and at the very widest and highest level we wish to raise the standard in the British Isles. In other words a real and lasting transformation of performance at all levels through coaching.

It may seem a simple aim, but in reality, of course, it is a long and difficult job because all the time we must judge any improvement against other school and club sides, counties and international sides, and even then we will not improve at all unless we can identify as a player, captain, coach or selector, the key factors. Having identified these key factors, for success and transformation of performance, all efforts must be co-ordinated and a long-range plan drawn up.

We are not quite at the end yet (or should I say beginning) for in progressive planning we must periodically take stock, in this case yearly, of our achievements and shortcomings so that we can if necessary realign our aim (The feed-back). You will note that figure 2 shows five-year plans from 1970 to 1974 and 1971 to 1975, and the years 1974 in the first plan or projection and 1975 in the second indicate those in which you should reap the reward of your planning and organization.

Although injuries, players moving to another area, and a loss of form, will affect the plan, this does not minimize the importance of having one. If anything it further emphasizes the part that thought, vision, continuity and action must play in any coaching set-up.

Above all else you must stress the need for demanding high standards. You should be working to your projected model and nothing short of absolute perfection (100%) will do. Schoolmasters, players and club coaches can be too easily satisfied and by the same token they can be insatiable. Everyone must strive to the maximum of their ability and coaches must discover what that maximum is.

5

Key Factors and Summary Chart

Now that we are thinking correctly and are working towards a framework (within which the detail will operate), it is time to outline the ten key factors which should guide our actions both on and off the field of play if we wish to attain the desired transformation.

In the first place we operate in an area of maximum size, 110 yards by 75 yards; the space that we have at our disposal is therefore clearly defined. Into this area we must fit thirty players and one referee and, at the time of writing, ask each and everyone of them to have a thorough understanding of the twenty-seven laws of the game. Throw in amongst this array of human endeavour, a ball, oval in shape, with a specified length, circumference and weight, point out the ' Object of the Game ' namely:

' The object of the game is that two teams of fifteen players each, observing fair play according to the Laws and a sporting spirit, should by carrying, passing and kicking the ball, score as many points as possible, the team scoring the greater number of points to be the winner of the match,' and you have your game of Rugby Union Football.

Or do you? Well, it is not quite as simple as that, because, as I pointed out in the opening chapter, the result will range from the superb spectacle of fifteen athletic men commanding the pitch to fifteen half-fit players stumbling and fumbling through eighty minutes of hell.

Therefore the ten key factors for the improvement of performance in attaining the above object must be understood and applied and here the player and coach in particular, should take note that these factors are the same at all levels.

c

For simplicity's sake, they are grouped under three main headings – attitudes, approach, and action. The importance attached to these headings is well illustrated by using the analogy of a three-legged stool. If there is anything wrong with one of the legs, then the stool falls over. It is maintained that the partial or complete failure of one or more of these factors appears to have a short or long term detrimental effect and vice-versa.

Attitudes

Quite often the difference between two sides can be summed up in one word – ATTITUDE. Whilst one side may want to win more than the other it is more than likely that this determination to win is the embodiment of the three key factors which are very much attitudes of mind.

Key factor number one is a POSITIVE TEAM attitude of mind. There can be no doubt that this stems from the coach and players' desire to implement the team concepts through each and every player realizing his own potential. This will result in the team playing attacking rugby in an attempt to score the maximum number of points. Variety is essential but only on top of the team concepts, for all efforts should be harnessed to the team. If the coach knows what he is doing then he will coach by exception so that natural ability and flair has every opportunity of displaying itself and not, as so often happens in bad coaching, gets stifled. Start by thinking in a positive fashion and harnessing your energy to the team.

As we saw in Chapter Two there is much misunderstanding over rugby terms and yet there is strong grounds for believing that terminology does breed attitudes. The use of the CORRECT TERMINOLOGY is therefore key factor number two.

The third and last key factor under the heading of attitudes, concerns the word PERFECTION. It has already been touched upon in the last chapter and it is of the utmost importance if the desired transformation at all levels is to take place. The word perfection is used in relation to the standards or degrees of dedication, discipline, respect for captain, coach, and game, mental and physical fitness, vision, and clear thinking, that are to be expected of the players, coaches, selectors and administrators.

In simple and easily recognizable terms it may mean arriving fit to practise, a full turn-out on a practice night, clean playing kit, respect for the spirit as well as the laws of the game. These and many other examples may seem of minor significance in isolation, but their total effect can be colossal. Some will no doubt say it is unreasonable to ask any rugby player or coach to strive for absolute perfection (100%) because it is unattainable.

This may be so, but if you are only aiming for 75% of perfection and some one else 100%, then there is every chance that they will do better than you, as neither of you are likely to attain absolute perfection. Having adopted the right attitude we move to the:

Approach

Key factor number four involves an understanding of the practical significance of the GAIN and TACKLE LINES. When

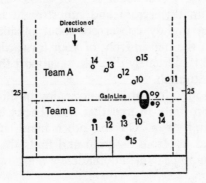

Figure 3

you step on a pitch, indeed whenever you practice as a team, make a mental note of where the try line is. It seems very obvious, but it is quite staggering how much effort is wasted in running across the pitch when the try lines are at either end of the playing area.

Look at Figure 3.

Here we have a typical situation in any game with, in this instance, team A ready to put the ball into the scrum. All being well, team A will gain quality possession of the ball and team B will come up on them as fast as possible to tackle and dispossess them of the ball. If they can, team A will cross this imaginary line, the gain line, before they are tackled – team B will be trying to make certain that they tackle and dispossess team A on team A's side of the gain line.

Now why is it important that team A should cross the gain line and that team B should stop them? Simply this: mistakes by team A either level with or behind their forwards will result in them not going forward, i.e. gain ground. (See Summary Chart pp. 48-9.) As a result team A's forwards will then have to run across the field or worse still, towards their own goal posts, before they can take part in the game again. (Law 24 – Offside.)

On the other hand, team B's forwards can pick their heads up from this scrum and run straight into the fray without being unduly concerned about offside. In simple English, ' Get the ball in front of your forwards ' otherwise they will find it extremely difficult to support the ball either quickly or in strength.

Psychologically, forwards do not enjoy pushing their guts out in a scrum only to find that their backs have made a mistake behind them. On the other hand, if a forward picks his head up from a scrum and finds that the ball is in front of him he will automatically start moving much faster.

The next question we should now ask ourselves is ' How

do we get the ball in front of our forwards?' There are obviously two simple ways:

(1) By running and handling, and
(2) By kicking.

Crossing the gain line by (1) RUNNING AND HANDLING. From the coach's point of view it is very easy to subdivide running and handling into moves involving (a) Penetrating your opponents' back line (running) and (b) Outflanking your opponents (running and handling).

A coach could well ask his boys or club backs to think of moves which will penetrate their opponents' back division or outflank their opponents, always bearing in mind these moves must be practised in relation to a gain line (you can use two corner flags or tracksuits to indicate what you have to cross) and that rarely in any one match would you have cause to use more than two or three well rehearsed moves. There is always the danger that backs, in their eagerness, will attempt too much and over-elaborate.

At the same time one should point out that there will be occasions in a game when you would wish to pass and run with the ball laterally in order to spread your opponents' defence, but as a general rule *the quicker you can cross the gain line and the nearer you can cross it to your forwards,* then obviously support from them will be on hand just that bit quicker and in greater numbers.

STRAIGHT RUNNING must play an important part if this key factor is to be applied in a game. Now what do we mean by straight running? It may literally mean running along a line parallel to the touchline. Every player has an opportunity of doing this during the course of a match, but for backs in particular the problem is quite acute especially as each back can expect an opponent coming in the opposite direction intent on destruction.

Of course, one must accept that the shortest distance be-

tween two points is a straight line, and backs will be trying
to run as straight as possible, or at least straightening out
at some point in their run, but a more realistic approach to
straight running is probably best illustrated by figures 4(a)
and 4(b).

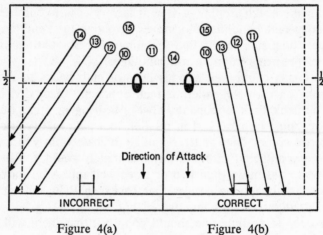

Figure 4(a)   Figure 4(b)

Crossing the gain line by (2) KICKING. It is extremely
easy to cross the gain line by kicking, any fool can do that,
but as I have already outlined, kicking means either losing
possession or giving your opponents a chance of regaining
possession. Therefore when you do kick in attack you should
do so on the premise that either yourself or a member of
your team *has a chance of getting the ball back again.*

If you bear this in mind you will realize how difficult a
skill kicking in fact is. You now have to decide not only
what sort of kick to use (high-hanging, chip through, screw
kick, etc) but where to place the ball. To illustrate this key
factor it is necessary to show certain tactics you might employ:

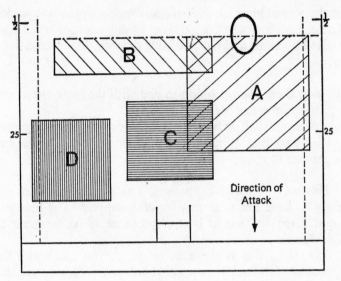

Figure 5

Look at each of these rectangular areas in the above figure as a guide to the places on your opponents' side where you might aim your kicks.

AREA A – is immediately in front of your forwards and therefore is the area in which you could expect maximum support from them. The blind-side wing threequarter can also be in this area very quickly to put the forwards on side if necessary. It is also a bad area for the opposition full back or right wing as both have little opportunity of doing much with the ball even if they catch it without the attention of opponents. It is rather like running into a cul-de-sac for the defence.

Best type of kick for your forwards – high and hanging: for your blind-side wing – low so that it rolls after pitching.

AREA B – this area is very definitely for the grubber kick

or the short chip kick over the advancing opposition backs. These are the sort of kicks you would attempt when confronted by a fast and hard tackling defence. You would hope to:

(a) stop them coming up on to you with the same speed and enthusiasm and/or
(b) place the ball between two of your opponents, or over them so that either yourself or one of your backs can run on to it.

This sort of tactic happens so quickly that you are unlikely to have much, if any, forward support. The best you could hope for would be the presence of your openside right flanker.

AREA C – this is the area in which you can make the opposition full back look a world beater (by kicking too low and too far) or else you can give him a most uncomfortable afternoon with high hanging kicks and consequently your forwards breathing down his neck. It is also very easy for your centres to reach this area.

AREA D – Not the area in which you can expect much support from your forwards for very obvious reasons, but most certainly you can expect your outside centre and wing to arrive soon after the ball, provided they know that the kick is coming. The kicker of a ball into this area should know that a screw kick normally pitches and rolls point over point and is easy to pick up on the run, whereas a punt could pitch and bounce in any direction.

The next point to consider on the ' gain and tackle line ' is the ALIGNMENT of the backs, which in turn is governed by another simple principle. The steeper you align then the further you have to run before you even reach the gain line. That is not to say that one type of alignment is preferred to another, because there are many other points to be taken into consideration. Some were mentioned under tactics in

Chapter Three and more again will be said when looking at the backs as a unit – Chapter Ten.

You cannot leave this important key factor without considering the importance of positional play and the need for being able to continually appreciate the total game situation. Every player on your team is given a position which he must be absolutely familiar with in all game situations. This would apply to both attack and defence.

A player out of position or not sure of his role is a luxury that a team can ill afford. Players must move to and from their positions as quickly as possible. An opponent on the ground is an opponent out of position and virtually out of the game, which means if you can get the ball in these circumstances then you could have a numerical superiority over the opposition and you should capitalize on this fact.

Finally, it should be clearly understood that an appreciation of the total game situation relies very much on (i) *every* player, not just the backs, understanding the real importance of the gain and tackle lines. Forwards should be just as orientated to keeping the ball in front of themselves as the backs are. (ii) Every player should act and react in unison with each other and this can only be achieved if communications are good. As will be seen on page 61 unless the forwards know where the ball is going after it has been won from a scrum they will never be able to support the man and ball successfully. Make certain you know what is happening!

Understanding the need for QUALITY POSSESSION is key factor number five. It can be a difficult game with the ball against skilled and determined opponents; without the ball, or with bad possession, it is an impossible one. However, not only do we need the ball; we need the ball at the right time and in the correct manner.

This we call QUALITY POSSESSION and it is distinguishable to any player from bad possession by a popular term in the game known as a hospital pass. If you have received a pass and an opponent at the same time, then you will appreciate the significance of the word ' hospital ' and the importance of receiving the ball at the right time and in the correct manner.

Quality possession is first of all striven for at scrums and line-outs, but there is a growing need for it from rucks, mauls and in general handling situations as the game becomes more fluid. Once you have this sort of possession then your team is in a position to dictate the play and naturally it follows that you must use the ball properly. In so doing you will retain possession of the ball by correct and accurate handling, by dribbling, by being able to pick the ball up on the run, by taking a tackle, by stopping forward rushes and of course by winning your own ball at scrums and line-outs. You should be aiming to keep the ball moving and the game fluid.

If your opponents have the ball then your job is to get it off them as quickly as possible, generally by determined tackling which forces your opponents into making errors. You should think twice about kicking because here you are either losing possession (kicking to an opponent) or giving them an opportunity to regain possession (if you kick into touch). I am not suggesting that you would think twice during the actual game, rarely do you have time for that, but you should realize the implications of putting your boot to the ball.

As a general rule the more efficiently the forwards can support each other in the scrum, line-out, ruck and mauls then the greater the chance of that team dominating the play and more in particular giving the game its aimed-for continuity. It also follows that the greater the number of supporting players and the closer they support each other in broken play then the greater the chance of your team being able to continue to move the ball towards the opponents' try line. Support for man and ball is therefore a very important aspect of winning quality possession.

I have already indicated that a man on the ground is a man out of the game, regardless of how quickly his reflexes may bring him back into a running position. This is never more apparent than in rucks where so often you see bodies all over the place and no ball in sight. Too often players, usually backs, abjectly surrender the ball or flop to the ground, when they should be fighting to stay on their feet so as to work the ball to a supporting player.

Again, if you are trying to get quality possession you will not do it lying on the ground and therefore the need for staying on your feet cannot be overstressed. It is very evident that every player must look upon himself as a potential provider of quality possession.

Selectors come in for some awful criticism at times and not without justification because the method of picking selectors may in itself be all wrong. As you will see in Chapter Six on Game Diagnosis, if a coach has to be a diagnostician then so have the selectors. Assuming the right selectors are in office then there ought to be no mistakes in team selection, but we know that the people best suited to select are not always in office and consequently the wrong team is picked.

SELECTION is therefore key factor number six and more needs to be said about it. Too often selectors are picked because: (a) they have given long service to a club; (b) they are the only ones available to attend selection meetings; (c) they are the only ones available to watch the various teams; (d) a certain club or area must be represented. Of course being able to attend meetings and watch various teams play is important, but other considerations should take precedent.

Selectors must be near enough to the game to keep their fingers on the pulse. Unless they have only recently retired from playing or have played an active part as a coach, then it is unlikely that they will be abreast of the times. They must have the coach's diagnostic ability or else they will be selecting and dropping players for the wrong reasons.

They must have an overall plan which reflects their positive approach to the game, and not the 'stop the opposition from scoring' attitude which is negative. Above all they must be prepared to be flexible, open-minded and bold in their selection policy.

Selection is a key factor and starts with the appointment of the selectors themselves and is then reflected in the choice of coach, captain and players. The whole approach to the appointment of selectors and the qualities that they need to carry out their vitally important task has tended to lag behind other developments in the game and there are still too many examples in club and county rugby, where the man who helps prepare the team (the coach) is not in fact a selector. An odd state of affairs.

Closely allied to selection is the need for the right sort of LEADERSHIP. Leadership, therefore, is key factor number seven and as we saw from the previous chapter the captain and coach play very important parts in how the teams react both on and off the field of play. You soon know if you have the right captain and coach by your own willingness to support their action. This also applies to the pack leader if he is not in fact the captain.

Another function of leadership is the diagnosis and correction of faults. The captain and coach should remember to diagnose and correct first the team, then the unit and lastly the individual. This order will ensure that the right perspective is being kept. A thorough knowledge of the laws of the game is also essential because a lack of knowledge can so often lose a match and by the same token, a thorough knowledge might help you to win.

For example, the offside law in open play is so often misunderstood and consequently penalty kicks are incurred as a result. An offside player standing within ten yards of an opponent waiting to catch the ball, has only one course of action, that is to move out of the area quickly. Standing with your hands in the air trying to convince the referee that you have no evil intentions will do you no good whatsoever. Leadership which is aware of these points will command respect and this sort of leadership is a precious commodity.

Before leaving the four key factors that govern our approach on and off the field of play the importance of mental and physical fitness must be mentioned. Many would argue that it is a key factor in its own right and whilst not wishing to lessen its importance in any way, reacting to the many situations which develop on a rugby field and the need to be mentally and physically fit to cope with them can, and should be, incorporated in the preparation for the game under quality possession and gain and tackle lines.

It is accepted that if your brain and body do not function in unison, at speed and you are absolutely fit, then the individual, unit and team performance must suffer. You can have the most magnificent side-step imaginable, but unless you are fit and fast enough to put yourself in a position to demonstrate it, then it becomes a useless skill.

Bearing these points in mind the personal aspects of mental and physical fitness are dwelt upon more fully in Chapter Thirteen, whilst here the need to incorporate them as an integral part of a team practice session and not as a separate item, are stressed.

Action

The importance of this third heading should be very apparent because, even though you may have the right attitudes and approach, if the action you take is insufficient or wrong then the end product will be affected. The action is essentially threefold.

Key factor number eight is concerned with the understanding, general acceptance and implementation of the PHILOSOPHY and CONCEPTS of the game. These are the very reasons for and roots of the game, and unless every player, coach and selector is speaking a common language, no matter at what level he is involved, then the confusion will continue and progress will be spasmodic. The role of the coach, whether schoolmaster or club, is vital – players must be encouraged to respect the ethics of the game, think more about it and learn through activity.

As we saw from figure 2 on page 31, someone has to sit down and do some thinking in the initial stages. Key factor number nine is therefore the initial DIAGNOSIS and PLANNING which must cover a period of several years. Do not confuse it with the actual coaching programme; the latter will in fact be the outcome of the initial diagnosis and planning.

The tenth and last key factor is the tangible evidence of all that has preceded in this and the previous chapter; it is in fact the COACHING PROGRAMME. Any academic subject must show progression from a common base and the coaching programme is no different.

In addition it will probably have to cater for coaches as well as players. For example, in a school it may well be necessary for the master in charge of rugby to coach his other coaches how to coach. So often the best school coach takes the first fifteen and finds that the playing material that eventually finds its way to him is deficient in many skills which might reasonably have been covered in the first year.

The importance of coaching the other coaches should now be apparent. If the latter has taken place, then the coaching programme will reflect continuity, so that as boys or club players move from one team to another, they do so with relative ease, because everyone is talking the same language.

The need for continuity in the coaching programme is also apparent when a school or club coach leaves. A well implemented programme will take such an event in its stride, because someone will have been groomed to take over. There should be no sudden fall in the playing standard.

A coaching programme should also aim to motivate

players and this is particularly important at school level. Visits from rugby personalities, visits to good club and international matches are essential to complement the practical work of the programme. So often this part is completely overlooked and boys miss so much as a result. They need something to inspire them.

Note

1 The ten key factors that have been listed in this chapter are only suggestions, but it would be well to remember that they cannot be added to willy nilly. On the other hand, if this number can be reduced, so much the better as we can then spend our valuable time on less key factors for success. It must be appreciated that the identification of the key factors is crucial.

2 Always check to see that you are not confusing the ' means ' to an end with the ' end ' itself. If you remember that the ' means ' are more akin to the ability and potential of the players, the time that can be spared for the game, and the degree of action taken, then you will have no problem in deciding what is a key factor and what is not. This approach can also be applied when working out the key coaching points. There is little point in giving unnecessary instruction.

You will see how the Summary Chart on the following pages draws everything together.

Summary Chart

KEY FACTORS	EXPLANATION AND IMPLICATION	KEY COACHING POINTS	PAGE REFERENCES
Attitudes 1. A Positive Team attitude	(a) All efforts should be channelled to the Team – 14 men working to make the 15th man's job easier.	The following are intended as examples only: (a) Coach by exception.	12, 13, 17, 21, 22, 34, 41, 58, 66-8,
	(b) Individual 'skill' and 'flair' have more chance of working successfully *within* a team frame-work than outside it.	(b) Encourage collective responsibility. (c) ATTACK is the best method of defence.	109, 117, 153, 181
2. Correct Terminology	(a) Use the accepted and correct terminology.	(a) FLANKER not wing forward. (b) PRACTICE = a session using the ball and incorporating Individual, Unit and Team skills. TRAINING = physical fitness.	14, 17-21. 32, 34, 35, 180, 181
	(b) 'Terminology breeds attitude'. '*Correct* terminology breeds *correct* attitudes'.		
3. Perfection	(a) Your 'model' should be 100% perfection. Aiming at anything less will do you less than justice.	(a) Aim for – whole Team at a practice session. Everyone to arrive FIT to PRACTISE etc.	18, 20, 21, 32, 34, 35, 67, 95, 181
Approach 4. Gain and Tackle Lines	(a) Imaginary lines of great importance – they tell you whether or not you are playing the game *behind* or *in front of* your forwards. The *latter* is necessary.	(a) Get the ball *in front of* the forwards. (b) Run straight. (c) Don't kick away quality possession.	35-41, 51, 52, 67, 96, 105, 109, 122, 130
5. Quality Possession	(a) Correctly timed feeding of the ball from all situations.	*Handling* (a) Carry the ball in two hands. (b) Ball out in front of receiver.	41-3, 53, 61, 64, 67-89, 90
	(b) With QP you can dictate the course of a game – without it the opposition can.	(c) Take the ball early – basic pass.	

		Ruck	101, 101, 126
		(a) Support in numbers. (b) Shoulder contact. (c) Drive opposition over gain line. (d) Stay on your feet. (e) Make the ball available.	
6. Selection	(a) Electing the right people to run the affairs of a school, club, etc. (b) From positive and intelligent selection all else stems.	(a) Are the right people in the right positions at club, country, etc, level?	23, 43, 44, 50-3, 170, 171
7. Leadership	(a) The ability to translate words into actions. It will take on many guises as there are many ways of leading and many different types of leader.	(a) Know the Laws, the game, the people! (b) Be able to *motivate*.	14, 22-5, 33, 44, 46, 50-3, 58, 66, 104, 129
Action 8. Philosophy and concepts	(a) These are the very reasons for and roots of the game. (b) They must be understood and implemented for maximum success and enjoyment.	Once the need for them is understood, then all they require is ACTION.	23, 34, 45, 46 59, 167
9. Diagnosis and Planning	(a) The insight and planning which should take place before KF No 10, and which should be projected over a minimum period of 3 to 5 years.		25, 29-31, 46, 57, 58, 164-6, 172-4
10. Coaching Programme	(a) Get it down on paper! prepare thoroughly; this includes the long term programme as well as every practice session. (b) The *tangible* outcome of KF No 9 incorporating progression continuity and motivation.	(a) Get it down on paper! prepare thoroughly; this includes the long term programme as well as every practice session.	23-5, 43, 46, 157-63, 164-6, 170-4

D

6

Game Diagnosis

Key factor number seven indicated that one of the attributes of a coach should be his ability to diagnose a game effectively. By this I mean he should be able on the one hand to see what is going right or wrong and on the other, be able to remedy any faults. I would suggest that plenty of people are capable of deciding what is going wrong, but few would know how to remedy the fault.

A player who is dropping the ball on almost every occasion will be abundantly obvious to one and all, but what will be less obvious is why he is dropping the ball and especially what steps should be taken to eliminate this sort of error. It is the difference between observing secondary effects and primary causes and this, in part, is the diagnostic ability that is required of the good coach.

Whilst the key factors are fresh in the reader's mind, the following might serve as a guide to watching a game with more purpose.

There is a great temptation to view a rugby match purely as a cinema show, with images flashing by and your eyes following the ball everywhere. Whilst obviously you must do this on many occasions, there is also much to be learned from watching players who have not got the ball, players who are perhaps picking themselves up from a scrum, and players who are walking.

At the end of the match, not only should you have a mental picture of how the game flowed, whether your side was principally attacking or defending, but you should also know why you lost the scrums or line-outs and what action you will take at your next practice session.

Quite obviously you cannot watch everything that is happening in any one match, nor should you attempt to, but you should systematically take your team's game apart over a period of time and know exactly its strengths and weaknesses. You should also look for weaknesses in the play of your opponents and, more important, know how to exploit them.

Probably the best position of all would be to have a helicopter view of the game, but as this is quite impractical you must do the next best thing and alternately view the game from the side and end of the pitch.

The immortal Adrian Stoop is reputed to have sat for match after match in the North Stand at Twickenham, because in his opinion this was the only position where he got a satisfactory view of the back play. I am convinced that this is absolutely right, because the running lines of the backs in both attack and defence are crystal clear from this position. You can soon tell why a centre is beating his opposite number, whether the backs are running across the field or straight up and down. Quite suddenly you realize what you have been missing by always viewing the match from the side.

On most grounds there is no problem in changing your viewing position, but even if there is, get a fellow selector to take one end and yourself a side or vice-versa; at the end of the match you will then be able to build up a very much more accurate picture of what happened and why it happened.

Bearing this in mind the following observations are intended purely as a guide to help the coach or selector to watch a game with some specific purpose in mind.

Points you might look for when viewing from the side.
1 Gain and tackle Lines: Do the team understand their importance?
2 Alignment of backs: Steep or shallow? Do they move together?
3 Kicking – effective or ineffective? Where? By whom?

4   Space, Scan, Switch – overall continuity of the game. Is
     it good or bad?
5   Is QP being obtained from:
     Scrum – Snap shove? Flankers packing down at the
     same time as the locks?
     Line-out – Jumper and wedges going forward? Scrum
     half correctly positioned to get his pass out?
     Ruck – Forwards fast enough to the break down
     point? Is there a platform? Never go in empty
     handed? Turning too early?
     Maul – Ball being screened?
6   Support in the scrum, line-out, ruck and maul.
     Does everyone seem to know their job? In attack as
     well as defence? Shoulder contact in support? Forwards
     supporting on each other's hips? First or last to line-
     outs?
     Where do attacks start? Own half? Opposition's?
     Counter-attack?

Points to look for when viewing end on.
1   Handling – Are the backs 'taking the ball early?'
2   Straight running
     Backs – to cross gain line.
     Coming up on the inside of their opposite numbers?
     Outside half has his chest facing you? Or shoulder?
     Forwards – Into rucks, parallel to the touch line?
     In general play do they keep movements going
     straight?
3   Variations
     Backs – Alignment and approach of players taking
     the ball in a switch.
     Forwards – Screening the ball, shoulder going in?
     Support – Positional play in attack and defence. Is the
     blind side wing covering? No 8 forward, where does
     he cover? Scrum – channels? Flankers wide enough?
     Scrum half one yard from scrum?

As I have indicated these questions are only guides and you can obviously add many more at your leisure.

It may also be a very worthwhile exercise to keep a count of the number of scrums, line-outs, rucks and mauls you win or lose and in particular whether it was quality possession or bad ball that you got. Even to observe or collect any of this information a pencil and notebook will not go amiss, because it is remarkably difficult to remember small, but probably important items a few days later when you are preparing the school or club practice session.

Remember you are looking for primary causes and not just secondary effects.

Game Breakdown

7

Team Play

Gone are the days when fifteen players could meet for the first time on a Saturday afternoon in the club dressing room, discuss a few possible moves and then go out and trounce the opposition. Playing effectively as a team demands tremendous team planning, and the more thorough the planning, then the less chance there is of things going wrong. Whoever started the ball rolling, started something which cannot be stopped.

No ambitious player can afford not to turn up to practice sessions, no club, county or country can afford not to get its players together to practise as a team; that is if it wishes to compete on an equal footing with its competitors.

The planning that is so integral a part of team play may, as I've already pointed out, be undertaken by the coach or by the coach and captain, but whoever does it, the important thing is that it must be done, and done systematically. It is worth repeating that it would be quite wrong for the coach to merely rely on his own personal experiences. Of course, these experiences may be of immense value, but the planning must reflect the coach's progressive thinking and his diagnostic ability. (See Summary Chart.)

In seeking to co-ordinate and blend the individual players into a team the following three factors must be taken into account because the optimum performance of any individual player, and consequently the team, is dependent on the amount to which these three inter-dependent factors have been developed.

(1) The player's skill and technique

(2) His overall understanding of the game, and his ability
     to interpret the changes that take place during the game.
     This is probably connected with his intelligence.
(3) Mental and physical fitness.

You will see quite clearly why they are inter-dependent – a
limitation in one will affect the others.

To the above three we must add the following, which may
not initially seem particularly relevant, but which in fact are
just as important and just as inter-dependent.

(4) Whether the players like each other and are prepared
     to work for each other.
(5) Whether they get the right sort of leadership from cap-
     tain and coach.
(6) Whether they are organized and practise together as a
     team.

In the first three points we have the platform of individual
competence upon which we begin to build our team. Next
we must consider the human relationships within the team
of players (points four and five) and finally make certain
that someone is competent enough to be master-minding the
overall plan and can see that it is systematically carried out
(point six). From this it should be abundantly obvious that
playing together as a team is not a simple question of
memorizing a few set moves. The integral parts of team play
go much deeper than this and this is why producing a successful side is so difficult – one weak link in the chain and
all around you crumbles to bits.

By successful side I mean (a) a winning one, and (b) one
in which the means by which the games are won are to the
liking of both players and spectators. How therefore do the
captain and coach produce a successful side?

I am sure there is no model answer to this question, but

the following approach to a school or club practice session may prove helpful.

In the first place the players have to accept the concepts and framework and this may require a certain amount of indoctrination from the coach. Naturally, the language used will be appropriate to the age and intelligence of the players. You would not dream of using the same language to a relatively experienced player of twenty-one as you would to a novice of eleven; the latter would not understand you. Yet, the concepts and framework should be identical.

Next you would involve them in the actual details of the game, ruck, maul, etc, remembering to harness their ideas and flair to the framework. The following suggestions as to the actual contents of a session may prove helpful.

Bearing in mind that a team is trying to score tries by keeping the ball moving and reduce stoppages through error to the minimum, then the key to a fruitful practice session is insisting on the maximum movement of the ball through handling. All the talking should be done in the changing rooms, once you get outside let the ball do the talking. Too often the bad coach gives himself, say twenty minutes, to practise line-outs and finds that ten to fifteen minutes of it is wasted through arguments over signals or how to wedge in on the jumper or the inability of the wing to throw-in accurately.

In the first place the signals should have been sorted out long ago, as should the method of wedging and if the winger cannot throw accurately over the required distance, as a temporary measure, bring him nearer to the forwards. If the object of the twenty minute practice was to have line-outs then at least sixty should take place. The wing can practise his throwing-in during his own time.

Similarly, if you want to practise scrumming, find opposition or a scrummage machine. In school it is simple on a games afternoon to arrange a rota for scrum practice, so that each team in turn gets a solid twenty minutes workout.

If one pack is much superior to any other, then add players to the weak pack to even things out. Often in clubs the backs make excellent fodder for the first fifteen pack and it works wonders for the relationship between backs and forwards, because the former realize what an enormous struggle the forwards have to go through to win quality possession.

Many club sessions, because of the problems in getting players to arrive and start at the same time, often begin with touch rugby. This is a great pity, because touch rugby produces players who run across the field and this, particularly in the case of forwards, is useless. You can partly eradicate this fault by playing ' double-touch ' (a side is allowed two touches before the game stops; which means a quick-thinking player can go straight through a would-be tackler and still retain possession), but this is only in part a solution; the best remedy is to start with individual skill practices, under pressure, with the players that have arrived.

If, of course, getting players to arrive at the agreed time is no problem, then after a warm-up with the ball and incorporating individual skills it is customary to let the backs and forwards sort out their own problems for twenty minutes, leaving a good forty to sixty minutes for (a) unopposed or skeleton rugby; and (b) semi-opposed rugby. You might on occasions try (c) a conditioned team practice or game, and even (d) a short game.

Unopposed rugby has much to commend it in spite of the fact that one hears criticism from some players that it is boring. I suppose it is, if you do it twice a week for eight months of the year, but then no decent coach would allow this to happen. At least, not if he had a plan which he systematically carried out.

The beauty of unopposed rugby is that you can go through every possible attacking situation that you are likely to come across during a match and work out a simple pattern of play that best suits the material that you have available. It is also an excellent way of acquiring a high degree of physical fitness.

Your drills can be mastered because there is no opposition to spoil or frustrate your play. You can encourage support in the broken play and your rucking can be developed. The dangers of unopposed rugby are also obvious and if the coach is not a perfectionist then sloppy habits can be acquired.

Ask any forward from a line-out or a scrum if he knows in which direction the ball will be going when it has been won. Ask him if he knows what move his backs will be attempting with the ball. Unfortunately, most will not have a clue and yet it is so desperately important that they should. In unopposed rugby it is so easy to organize directional signals and also see if they are working. For example, the scrum half knows that the ball is going left when it has been won by his forwards from a scrum, because he has received a signal from his outside half to indicate this. Therefore,

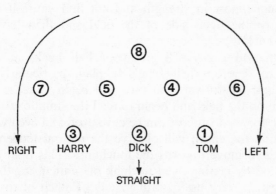

Figure 6 (Black Team)

The scrum half simply calls out 'Tom' pause – 'Blacks' – pause, 'Now' to indicate that the ball is going left. The other signals are obvious. Meanwhile, the coach should have positioned himself near to the scrum to hear the call and check that there has been a sufficient pause between the 'Tom' and 'Blacks' and 'Blacks' and 'Now' to give the forwards a chance to orientate themselves.

They now know in which direction to support and the coach would be well advised to urge the forwards to move briskly from the scrum to the next situation. If you waste as little as one or two seconds in getting from a scrum, a line-out, ruck or maul (probably by not knowing in which direction to support the ball) then this means that a ten to fifteen yards gap has developed between yourself and the next situation in which your support is required. In even more practical terms it means that three forwards will arrive at the breakdown point instead of eight.

Unopposed rugby can develop speed of thought and give excellent indication as to each individual player's physical speed and fitness. From the line-out a directional signal can be just as important, because if you know that your inside centre is going to kick the ball back to the blindside, then you can support in strength and not find yourself having moved to the open side of the field and then having to double back.

Unopposed rugby will give your half backs an opportunity to develop their blindside play, particularly from rucks, and the forwards in turn will begin to sense where they are on the field and begin to read the situation.

Close forward support can be developed and even without opposition the coach will observe the natural tendency for forwards to move towards the touchlines. This fault can be eradicated by getting them to think of running for the near goal post. A very useful drill that the French often use to encourage passing the ball inside may help you (figure 7).

With this drill, you can also encourage the sort of support where the ball is taken at hip height and each man accelerates through the ball simply by bringing the two lines of players closer together.

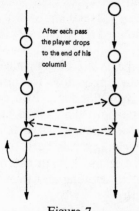

Figure 7

Forward support either with the ball in their hands or at their feet can be turned into rucks, as can cross-kicks that have been caught or when a player simulates a tackle.

Control of the ruck and improvement in technique can be acquired very simply by insisting that the ball is never released until at least six forwards have arrived. If it is a hand ruck, the man with the ball doesn't take his hands off it until he feels the weight coming from players arriving four and five. Six, seven and eight should not be far behind.

If the ruck has developed as a result of a simulated tackle, then the first three players up must get their front feet over the man and ball to form the platform. Players arriving fourth and fifth then really have something to drive into.

The loose forwards can try their moves from a scrum or the peel from a line-out. The backs can practise their moves until they are perfect and also the forwards can be turned against the backs with the dual purpose of checking whether the backs can stand up to pressure and whether the flankers and number eight forward are covering effectively. Kick-off, twenty-five drop outs, short penalties can all be rehearsed.

The coach should create as many situations as possible so that each and every player's knowledge and experience increases, but take note: everything should be done in relation to the gain line.

When you feel that your players have reached a satisfactory level without opposition, for instance they do not make mistakes in their handling, then now is the time to bring in a few opponents. There is a great temptation to practise line-outs, for example, against another eight forwards before the technique has been mastered. This is invariably a mistake, because human nature being what it is, someone will resort to spoiling and then no one gains anything from the practice.

The opposition must be told by the coach precisely what they can and cannot do. Using our line-out as the example again, you might begin by asking three or four opponents to try to get through your team's line-out – no jumping for the ball, just trying to get through the line-out. If these three or four opponents cannot get through the line-out, in other words the wedging is good, and legal, then bring in the rest of the opposition. Again begin by asking them to get through the line-out and now get your scrum half to move the ball away to his outside half.

If all is still going well, then reduce the number of players in the opposition line-out to three or four again, but this time let them jump for the ball. If you are given two packs of forwards to coach and you are practising rucks, mauls, line-outs, and scrums, make certain that both sides have an opportunity to practise and recognize getting quality possession from various playing positions, and also in defending.

There is a real danger that you will neglect the second or junior side and if you have injuries or if players lose their form then the second or junior players should be absolutely familiar with what is required of them when they step into the first fifteen.

What is also so often neglected in a practice session is

the skill of counter-attacking. The 'Dispensation Law', as it was originally called, has demonstrated very clearly that there are many occasions during the game when a ' running ' full back can completely alter the whole character of the match by counter-attacking.

The good coach can soon set up situations where the forwards take on the backs and the full back is faced by one or two flank forwards. This is also where we bring the wings into the game by making certain that the full back always has instant support on hand from one of them and the other takes over the covering role of the full back.

Ask any back who has played against a New Zealand or South African side where he would prefer to have the ball from. He will almost certainly tell you that he either wants the ball from the ruck or from broken play because his speed and flair can then be used. The ball from scrum or line-out, whilst invaluable, is very difficult to use against such tight and well organized defences. Do not neglect this aspect of the game, captains and coaches.

It is also important not to overburden the backs with full scale opposition from scrum and line-out situations until they are ready for it, but obviously they must have opposition at some point. Only you, the coach, can decide when that moment has arrived. The players want a very clear picture of what they are attempting to achieve and if by bringing in too many opponents too soon the practice never gets started, then nothing will be learnt.

Having now sorted out all our attacking plays and the role that each player has in every conceivable defensive situation you, the coach, may very well introduce the ' conditioned ' game.

The conditions you impose are entirely up to you; for example, you might indicate that there will be no kicking of any sort in your opponents' half; that for a set period of time one side will not strike for the ball in the scrums, everyone is to have their feet back and push; every penalty kick

E

must be taken with a short kick.

The scope is unlimited; the important thing is to impose a condition for a specific purpose which you feel will help to eradicate certain errors, make players back each other up and use the space around them, etc. If you also have to act as the referee, and this is very common, make certain that you are competent, otherwise once again the conditioned game will degenerate into a spoiling match.

All I would say about using a full scale game as a means of practising, is to use it sparingly. Apart from injuries that may occur and always at the wrong time, thirty players who know each other very well rarely gain much from such an activity.

Depending on the time that you have available your practice priorities would normally be: (i) Team and unit skills; (ii) Individual skills; (iii) Fitness, in this order.

If real benefit is to be gained from practising as a team there remains one final ingredient, and that is DISCIPLINE. Ideally, it would be self-discipline, but if a player is not pulling his weight, is in the wrong frame of mind and having a detrimental effect on the rest of his colleagues, captain and coach please do not hesitate, just ask him to leave the field and tell him to come back when he can control himself. He will!

It is only natural that all teams, their captains and coaches should strive for success and in part success obviously means winning. Unfortunately, there will aways be a lot of disappointments because everyone cannot win in spite of the fact that this will be their goal. Enjoyment and success are often synonymous, and hard work and discipline on the part of the players are the best ways of ensuring that they happen.

Finally, I feel that it should be re-emphasized that coaching and team work, far from stifling initiative, should and can afford each player far greater scope to employ his talents and flair to the full.

8
Forwards as a Unit

The hallmark of a highly organized and efficient pack of forwards is their apparent togetherness. They are everywhere the ball is and what is more a blanket could cover them, so closely are they supporting each other. I suppose every captain, club coach, and rugby master is striving to achieve this degree of unity and it will only be achieved with the right blend of players who should like each other and be prepared to help and work for each other so that the next man's task becomes just that bit easier. This support is not just concerned with broken play, but particularly in the scrum, line-out, rucks and mauls.

In discussing forward play it is so easy to get bogged down with detail and forget that the prime function of forward play is twofold, to get quality possession of the ball and then go forward by supporting the ball wherever it may be. Tries are bound to follow as a result of these two actions.

Normally one would begin by discussing the scrum and line-out, but these can keep. The changing emphasis from static forward play to dynamic forward play, from podgy immobile forwards to powerfully athletic forwards, demands that this point be tackled first.

Becoming more mobile is no great problem, all it requires is some self-discipline and dedication on the part of each individual forward. Everyone is capable of being more mobile simply by becoming fitter.

Having acquired the necessary mobility one needs to learn how to run or at least make contact, at the most advantageous angle. Advantageous in the sense that the shoulder makes contact first, thus knocking the opposition backwards, and secondly so that the ball is not trapped between players or smothered, but so that it can be made available to supporting players or else put on the ground ready to be rucked or driven over. I've already stressed that the ball belongs to the team and no one should die with it.

British forward support play has been characterized by its uprightness, whereas New Zealand and South African forward play has been noted for its closeness and the angle at which the players have leaned forward.

The British method has produced no forward drive; you cannot shift the opposition with your chest or stomach, and consequently rarely have British forwards managed to gather momentum as they supported each other. The end result has been a loose scrum or mêlée of players and the ball buried somewhere under them.

On the other hand the direct thrust of New Zealand and South African forwards, coupled with shoulder contact, has resulted in the ball nearly always being available for a forward in support of the ball or it being squirted back from a ruck or maul. Even when watching two New Zealand club sides, who are using identical techniques, the game flows because the ball is nearly always kept available and obviously the team going forward at that moment of time is the one that usually wins the ball.

Spectators are not the only ones who want to see the ball moving, players strangely enough are just as anxious.

The correct running angle does not just happen by accident; it has to be taught and coached in game situations. If one may generalize, I think British players instinctively think of ways of going round an opponent, whereas New Zealanders, in particular, accept that it is a contact game and, if an opponent is standing in front of them, the shoulder charge is the surest way of making progress to the opponents' goal line, or at least committing an opponent.

A balance between rounding an opponent and running

through him is called for, but this sort of reasoning does, I feel sure, account for the basic difference in angle of running that exists between players from New Zealand and players from the Home Unions.

Happily, there are signs, particularly England's tremendous forward performance against the 1969 South Africans, that attitudes are changing and so is the approach to the game. The consequent result will be a far freer flowing game, because the ball will be available much more.

The Ruck

The need for the correct running angle is even more accentuated when a player arrives at a ruck. You must drive into rucks hard and low; an upright approach is totally useless, because you will simply find yourself joining the mêlée of players in front of you without any forward drive, your head up in the air and consequently quite unable to see the ball, which naturally enough will be on the ground.

There has been a lot of talk about the ruck over the last few years, much of it ill-informed, so much so that players have gone on to the field with the need for creating rucks so much in their mind that the object of the game, to score more points than the opposition, has been forgotten. Players have even been seen turning to create a ruck in the middle of the field with not an opponent in sight. The ruck is important, but its function should be seen in the perspective of the whole game.

Indeed, there would rarely be any need to ruck the ball back if you could keep it moving to your opponents' goal line. (See Plate 1.)

The essence of the game is to support each other and, if the support is good, then tries must come at regular intervals. However, there must always come a moment of time when the ball-carrier cannot: (a) get any further; (b) give the ball to a player of his own team in a better position than himself, or (c) keep the play moving with a kick, if he deems this to be expedient.

When a player finds himself in a situation where these three conditions apply, then the ball should reach the ground behind him so that the rest of his forwards can ruck on to him and over the ball.

There is no mystery in rucking, no immensely difficult or complicated skill to be learned, the only real problem lies in getting eight forwards to the breakdown point. If you can achieve this, then it is a ten minute job to brush up your technique.

The key coaching points in rucking are:

(i)   Shoulder contact.
(ii)   Stay on your feet.
(iii) Never go in empty-handed.
(iv)   Make the ball visible to the support.
(v)   Always pack in on the far side first, to shorten the running distance of the next man up.
(vi)   Drive in parallel to the touchline, head down looking for the ball.
(vii) Walk over the ball, do not heel it; use the side of your foot.

Having digested the above coaching points, it is necessary to outline the technique in a little more detail, especially bearing in mind the schoolboy who will not find it easy to drive in, head down over the ball, unless he can be assured that he is physically safe. If he has doubts he will lose his momentum when he arrives at a ruck and deliberately stop with his head up in the clouds; in this positon he is neither of use nor ornament to his team.

Rucks normally develop round a player with the ball in his hands (hand ruck) or after a player has been tackled and the ball cannot be picked up and moved forward (foot ruck). Assuming the ball carrier finds himself in a situation where the conditions (a) (b) and (c) apply, then *if he wants maximum control over the ball,* he can try to turn and 'squeeze' the ball into the ground, thus forming a HAND RUCK.

Figure 8(a)   Figure 8(b)

He must keep on his feet – feet apart for a good base. Note his head is down.

Another type of hand ruck occurs where the ball-carrier finds it quite impossible to turn. It should make no difference so long as the ball is made available to the supporting players.

Figure 9

In figure 9 the ball has been slipped between the ball-carrier's legs and to the ground, so that it can now be seen by the forwards in support. Just look at Colin Meads in Plate 2 – note the angle at which he is running.

The next player up, regardless of his forward position, should bind on to and over the far side of the man with the ball. Player three to arrive should do the same on the near side of the first player. Both players two and three should be thinking of lifting the first man with their inside arms so that all three remain on their feet.

Figure 10(a)   Figure 10(b)

This is your PLATFORM – without it the ruck will end as a loose scrum of sprawling bodies. Players arriving fourth and fifth ideally would bind as they are arriving so that their combined drive moves the front three over the ball.

Figure 11(a)   Figure 11(b)

Figure 11(c)

Some coaches on the other hand prefer that players arriving fourth and fifth bind and drive on to the outside of players two and three respectively. They feel that this gives more width to the ruck and curbs opponents, who arrive late, from slipping round the side of the ruck (figure 13).

Player arriving sixth takes the No 8 position as in figure

Figure 12

12; or players arriving sixth and seventh pack as in figure 13.

Figure 13

If you are coaching players arriving fourth and fifth to drive on to the inside of players two and three, then you get maximum drive over the ball. If, on the other hand, you have a pack of forwards who all arrive together, then it matters little what permutation you employ.

Assuming players arriving fourth and fifth are packing on the inside of two and three and that the sixth player to arrive acts as a No 8 forward, then players arriving seventh and eighth act as flankers; or they could act as a scrum half or threequarter-back if any of those players are trapped in the ruck.

Figure 14

The schoolmaster coach would do well to point out that there is a place for everyone's head. Once confidence is acquired then a more dynamic ruck can be developed. There is also no point in bringing in full opposition until everybody is fully conversant with the eight positions that he could find himself in.

Let me just reiterate that there is a real danger of turning far too early and completely losing the forward momentum. You must aim to drive straight through an opponent. The turn only comes, if it is coming, after shoulder contact and when the ball carrier can get no further.

Foot Ruck

So often in teaching and coaching tackling we forget to

mention the ball. It is worth emphasizing again how important it is for the man carrying the ball to make certain that when he is tackled, the ball is made available to a supporting player. At worst he should make certain that he hits the ground with his body between the ball and the opposition – his own team then have some chance of winning any ensuing ruck.

Now rightly the law points out that a man who has been tackled should roll away from the ball, but the law respects that at times it is quite impossible to do this and if our forward support is perfect then no sooner will the tackled player have hit the ground than his forwards will have arrived. Again, assuming that we have been mentally geared to picking up the ball beforehand, but have failed or have been unable to do so, then and only then does the following drill for a foot ruck take place.

Figure 15(a)   Figure 15(b)   Figure 15(c)

(i) The first to arrive puts his foot and body well astride of man and ball facing forwards.

(ii) The second player packs in on him, remembering to take the far side first.

(iii) The third player to arrive raises his inside arm and packs over the first man, on the near side.

In other words, it is the same build-up as for the hand ruck.

A few of the coaching points should be re-emphasized at

this point. *Keep on your feet by walking over the ball.* If the first three to the breakdown point fall flat on their faces, then everyone coming behind will have nothing to drive into and so they will also end up in a heap. The need for the first three players to form a platform is of paramount importance. One should also remember that 'a man on the ground is a man out of the game'.

Maul

The laws tell us that in a ruck the ball is on the ground and in a maul the ball is held in the hand. From my description of the ruck it is equally obvious that a maul may turn into a ruck, but not vice-versa; the latter would incur a penalty for handling in a ruck. In broken play the offside line for a ruck and a maul is the same, namely the hindmost foot of the last player in the ruck or maul, and therefore many sides practise almost identical techniques for both these phases of the game.

Figure 16

It is obvious from figure 16 what has happened. This sort of maul has some shape and recognizable pattern to it; on other occasions when we say a maul is taking place, what we are usually confronted with is a jungle of players with the ball being smuggled from hand to hand until someone tears himself free and feeds the ball to a scrum half or else makes off with the ball in the direction of the opponents' goal line.

The systematic build-up to the ruck and maul that I have previously outlined, and not the latter haphazard affair, can be used when receiving kick-offs, twenty-five drop-outs and as a line-out variation in either a defensive or preferably an attacking position.

When considering defence round a ruck or maul the onus falls on those two players who find themselves on either flank, to pincer on to the opposition scrum half as flankers in a scrum would do. There is no problem if you are going forward at the moment of time when the ruck or maul takes place, because you should win the ball.

On the other hand, when you are going backwards this is when those on either flank of the ruck or maul need to be wide awake; especially the player who finds himself with the short or blind side of the field to defend.

Having now looked at some methods of maintaining possession of the ball it is time to see how quality possession can be won from line-outs and scrums.

Line-out

Although a line-out is simply a means of re-starting the game, the importance of winning quality possession of the ball from the line-out should not be underestimated, as most games have on average fifty to sixty line-outs.

Again there are two gross misconceptions about line-out play which must be eradicated immediately. Unfortunately, it is not one member of a team versus his opposite number, but your eight forwards plus scrum half and thrower-in against, you hope, the opposition's jumper. Let's just explain this statement. Year in, year out, the British Isles have produced jumpers with hands like leeches and the ability to leap into the air like Nureyev.

Although they might have looked marvellous going up for the ball and even managed to catch it in two hands, so little of the ball has found its way into the scrum half's hands. Why? Principally because they have lacked support from the rest of their forward unit. Mind you, the jumping has not always been aggressive, but essentially the trouble has been in weak and badly timed wedging and generally so much space has been left between players in the line-out that a double-decker bus, let alone the opposition forwards, could have driven through it.

Of course, some sides have made giant strides in the organization of their line-outs, but players generally are still too narrow-minded in their thinking and slow in their reactions.

' I'm a prop,' they say, ' so I don't gather the ball.' ' I'm a flanker, so neither do I.' To an obvious extent they are correct because it is pointless if everyone jumps for the ball, but you will notice that I used the word ' gather ' and not ' jump ' in the two examples above, because, and this is the second misconception, every forward is a potential gatherer of the ball.

In a line-out everyone must be completely flexible. You, as a forward, know only too well how few players can throw the ball in accurately, so bearing this in mind, you must keep your eyes on the ball at all times and be prepared to gather it and give your scrum half quality possession.

Before the ball is thrown into a line-out there should be two signals. The first, probably from the scrum half or pack leader, should indicate to the man throwing in the ball exactly where it is to go and perhaps what type of line-out it will be, and the second signal should indicate in which direction the ball will be going when quality possession has been won. This last signal should also be given before the ball has been thrown in.

The man throwing in the ball should hold it above head height, you should know why, and the line-out is ready to begin.

Normally line-outs fall into two categories (a) Wedge or

Feed; (b) Ruck or Drive. In type (a) the ball is usually fed to the scrum half by the jumper, or whoever ultimately gathers the ball. (See Plate 3.)

In type (b) the ball is caught, put on to the ground, and the forwards take up a ruck formation and drive over the ball. The latter type often presents problems for the opposition loose forwards because they either have to be a part of the ruck or behind the hindmost foot of the last player on their side of the ruck. This gives your half backs time to manoeuvre. Most line-outs quite obviously take place right up to the five yard line and these are the ones I shall look at right now.

WEDGE OR FEED. The success of this type of line-out depends on the players on either side of the jumper wedging in on him and taking him forward. Make certain you have read and understood Law 23! The rest of the forwards can take part in the wedge as well, providing their feet are behind the ball. See figure 18(a) (b) for two ways of wedging.

In figure 18(a) (b) apart from the two players forming the normal wedge on to the jumper, the rest of the players would normally be so close together that none of the opposition could get through the line-out during the split second it took the jumper to catch the ball and feed it.

It is up to the last player in the line-out to push the other forwards up tight on to the five yard line before the line-out starts; this will ensure that no gaps are left in the line-out.

RUCK OR DRIVE. As a general rule teams employ the previous line-out method if they are going to run with the ball and in particular they feed from positions five to eight, which has the principal advantage of committing the loose forwards at the end of the opposition's line-out.

On the other hand, the ruck or drive type of line-out is usually used purely as a defensive measure, where the ball is thrown to players standing at two or three in the line-out. This, I feel, is a great pity because, given adequate practice, its use as an attacking line-out with the ball being thrown to five, six, seven or eight, has enormous possibilities for the attacking team, which will then have two sides of the field in which to manoeuvre, instead of the usual one.

RUCK OR DRIVE AT THREE

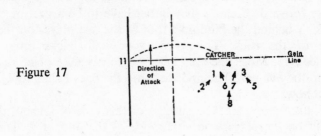

Figure 17

RUCK OR DRIVE AT FIVE AND SEVEN

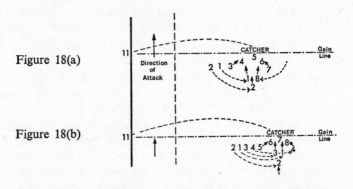

Figure 18(a)

Figure 18(b)

NOTE – the ruck at three, five and seven refers to the position in the line-out where the player stands and not necessarily the number on his back.

If you have an excellent thrower in, then the whole line-out can be taken in field a further five to ten yards. The opposition will probably spread their line-out and leave your eight forwards against five or six of the opposition; the other opposition forwards standing in the space you have left up to the five yard line.

Remember if you can catch and ruck the ball, the opposition in the space at the front must either join the ruck or get behind the hindmost foot, otherwise they will be offside.

There are, of course, other types of line-out, four-man line-outs; split line-outs; and long-stretched line-outs. With adequate practice they will all work, but it is difficult to achieve much from them without this. Their principal value is that they tend to break up the opposition's pattern and they may, on occasions, so disorganize them that when you next have an orthodox eight-man line-out you catch them not concentrating and so win the ball.

What catches more forwards out than anything else is the team that takes quick line-outs either when only two or three of the opposition have arrived or the long throw-in when the forwards have just had to dash from one side of the field to the other. Psychologically they are anticipating getting their breath back and if someone throws a long ball over the end of the line-out just as they have arrived you will catch them all flat-footed.

Do remember that your own side must know that this sort of thing can happen or else you will be most unpopular. You should also bear in mind that it is better to attack from the middle and end of the line-out than the front, because the ball at the middle and more so the end of the line-out, will engage the opposition loose forwards and thus give your own half backs more time and room in which to operate.

Of course, one must anticipate that the opposition will also get the ball and that is why all the binding shown in this book, quite clearly shows the players pointing in the direction in which they are playing. There will be occasions when you find yourself with your back to the opposition but these will be few and far between – perhaps on the odd occasion when the ball is being fed to your scrum half. By facing the opposition you are ideally placed to get through the line-out

F

and on to their scrum half. If the ball has been lost and is now on its way towards your own goal line then you have to cover. Figure 19 will give you a guide as to the direction you might take.

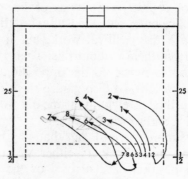

Figure 19

The word 'guide' should be stressed because I do not think you can lay down any hard and fast rules; after all the forwards should be striving to get to the breakdown point as quickly as possible.

If each individual forward in the line-out knows his job and is able to carry it out, bearing in mind that he must be flexible enough to cope with the many varied situations which do arise as a result of bad throwing in, then the important task of winning quality possession will be achieved.

Scrum

Few sides these days use the 3:2:3 scrum, where the weight is concentrated on the opposition hooker. Everyone seems to favour the 3:4:1 formation because they feel it gives a more comfortable and effective forward drive if everyone knows what he is trying to achieve and applies his weight at the same time. Weight is applied in the following directions.

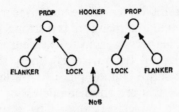

Figure 20

As you will see the two locks are applying the bulk of their weight via their outer shoulder through the inner buttock of the prop on their side of the scrum and the flankers are applying their weight via their inside shoulder through the outside buttock of the respective prop. Quite obviously some weight must be going on to the hooker, but relatively little as compared with the 3:2:3 scrum. In the 3:4:1 scrum it should be very apparent why it is necessary for the flankers to pack down at the same time as the locks. As you will see from the line of force, the props will be pushed outwards, thus losing contact with the hookers unless the flankers do their job properly.

When looking at the forwards as individuals, the importance of correct binding (pulling with your arms) is stressed as is the importance of the locks and No 8 forward being able to lock the scrum when the ball has been won. In this latter respect, the three forwards concerned should look at the following figures:

Figure 21(a) (Incorrect)   Figure 21(b) (Correct)

The correct method is less tiring and gives much more purchase on the ground and therefore is a stronger position for:
(a) executing a snap-shove, and (b) locking the scrum.

Quite obviously all the forwards' knees should be bent
prior to a 'snap-shove' taking place. If we look at a scrum
from the side we will see another interesting feature which
helps to create a top-class scrum. The scrum gets lower
from front to back. There is no effective forward drive from
humpty-backed locks – remember the coaching tip for these
players? 'Drop your knees.' Basically there are three
channels in a scrum through which the ball can come and
they are as follows:

Number One

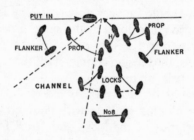

Figure 22

A ball picked up by the scrum half from this channel, has
had the shortest route to take and can often result in a very
quick ball. However, too often coaches condemn this pick-
up area because their scrum half is continually being caught
by his opposite number. They then decide that they will only
have the ball from between the No 8 forward's feet or to the
right of him as they feel this is safe.

Maybe it is, but it also produces a much slower ball and
of course gives the opposition backs in particular, time to

move up ready to tackle their opposite numbers. Coaches also condemn this pick-up area if the ball shoots right out of the scrum and their scrum half has to chase after it.

The answer lies not in changing the pick-up area, but in making certain that the scrum half is one yard away from the scrum and that the actual put-in and hooker strike or deflection are practised until the ball can be delivered exactly to the fringe of the pick-up area. In other words, if your forwards cannot do this then they are not functioning as a unit.

Number Two

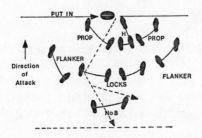

Figure 23

With the ball being channelled to the No 8's feet or to the right of him, the hooker must first of all deflect the ball closer to the left lock who in turn can then bring his own left foot forward and drag the ball back to the No 8. It is very simple from there.

The left flanker would either pack wider to make the opposition scrum half take a longer journey, or closer to the left lock to make certain that the ball did not shoot straight out of the scrum. A ball being channelled to this position is definitely a fraction slower than being channelled to the first position, but on the other hand it does gives the scrum half a lot of protection.

Number Three

To use this channel properly, that is from which an attack might spring, it is best to pack down 3:3:2 thus:

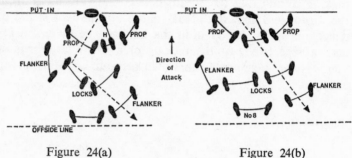

Figure 24(a)   Figure 24(b)

You will see that both locks have reversed their feet position (in figure 24(a)), that is, their inside feet are now back and their outside feet forward. The left lock deflects the ball across the scrum to the right of the flanker, who is now packing on to the right lock, and level with the No 8 forward.

There should be no problems in connection with the scrum offside line and the flanker is in a good position from which to attack, especially if he has support from his No 8 and scrum half.

Many of the other points concerned with the scrum will be covered in the next chapter, when discussing the forwards as individuals. Make certain that every forward knows what is happening before the ball goes in, and in which direction the ball is going, whether it has been won or lost. Everyone must be comfortable, otherwise the scrum will never function as a cohesive unit.

Therefore, feet positions and binding must be attended to, as well as the position of the chin. If a forward's chin is on his chest, then his back will be round; if his chin is up, then his back will be flat, and this is what it should be. The snap-shove must be practised and so must locking the scrum, otherwise the forwards are always going to be struggling to get the ball, let alone win quality possession.

The Wheel

Do not confuse the constructive ploy of deliberately wheeling the scrum for the purpose of starting a foot rush (dribble) with either the deliberate turning of an opponent's scrum or the accidental slewing of a scrum, which occasionally happens if one set of forwards is very much weaker than another.

We know that the natural way for a scrum to turn is towards the loose head side, and in a wheel this fact is made use of. You obviously must have a weight advantage over your opponents or else the chances of the wheel working are next to nothing.

Assuming this is the case, then the wheel, whilst prearranged, should only take place after the ball has been won and held in the second row by the left-lock. You do not put the ball into the scrum and start the wheel. The ball is won, held by the left lock and then everyone takes part in the wheel on the prearranged signal.

The tight head prop helps by easing himself backwards and the right flanker pushes on to the tight head prop and the right lock. The locks are pushing diagonally left towards the loose head side and at the same time easing their shoulders and heads out from between the props.

The end result is that the opposition have been successfully wheeled right out of the path of the two locks and No 8 forward, who advance with the ball at their feet.

Rarely do you see this skill today because packs seem to be either so well matched, or they have not bothered to practise it.

Defence round the scrum

This drawing only shows the forwards, but quite obviously

the outside half and scrum half, particularly the former, have very important jobs to do in relation to defence round the scrum.

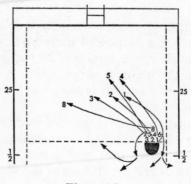

Figure 25

Again these lines are intended purely as a guide; the only ones which have modified and become deeply appreciated over the years, concern players six, seven and eight. The reasons are outlined in the next chapter.

Receiving a kick-off

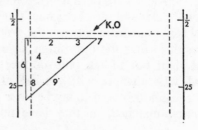

Figure 26

The player moving into the ball takes it.

Receiving a 25 yard drop out

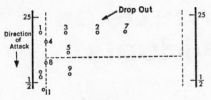

Figure 27

Here I have shown a flanker and the hooker standing up to the twenty-five yard line with one on either side of the kicker. This is not absolutely necessary, one man will often do, but you must make sure that the drop out in fact goes to your forwards – you then have a chance of regaining possession.

Facing a kick at your own goal

At least one forward must be appointed to face his own goal posts in order to take any ricochet. Other situations involving the forwards do occur; for example – if the opposition ' mark ' the ball then it is usual to stand your two locks on the mark, hoping that their long arms might charge down the free kick.

If a penalty has been given against your team, then one forward at least should always keep his eye on the ball and go for the opponent who takes the short penalty.

In any event, all players, and forwards in particular, should retire the ten yards that the law requires as quickly as possible and keeping a close watch on what is happening. Try not to turn your back on the ball.

Remember – *forwards win matches*.

9

Forwards as Individuals

Having stressed the importance of every player knowing his role in the team context, we look a little more deeply at the individual forwards, the players who win matches.

More is expected of forwards these days than ever before and gone are the days when the glory went entirely to the backs. Test this statement out on probably the most powerful and awe-inspiring team of the last twenty years, the 1967 All Blacks, and just jot down the number of their forwards you can still remember as opposed to their backs.

British forwards are slowly learning that their job is not just concerned with gaining quality possesion, but supporting the ball in all phases of the game. There is no earthly reason why a prop forward or a lock could not, indeed should not, play in the backs with as much skill as the more usual occupants.

Forwards should not be slow and ponderous, be incapable of stooping down to pick the ball off the ground, or have wooden hands, they should be footballers in the widest sense of the word – in fact, because of the increased demands being asked of them it is essential that they should be truly skilful players.

The Loose forwards

Flankers and No 8 Forward

Although three players are embodied in the term loose forwards, their roles are so closely interwoven that there is every justification for looking at them as a group. Not only are they concerned with the scrum and line-out, but their play in the loose is of vital importance – they are the link players between the forwards and the backs. The very old, yet true, maxim, *a good big 'un will always beat a good little 'un* can very much be applied to these three.

I am sure it is no accident that New Zealand and South African flankers have been big mobile men, who have been able to use their weight in the scrums, their strength in the mauls and their speed to get to the loose ball. (See Plate 4.) Think of the traditional British flanker. Generally he has been quick, destructive, but very light by comparison.

The situation is changing, of course, possibly because of law changes, which have in turn made sides adopt the 3:4:1 scrum, and also because schoolmasters, club coaches and selectors have seen the value of having big men at the back of the line-out, and men who can use their bulk in the loose.

Whilst our flankers are getting bigger and stronger and are well able to use their hands they are in many cases still trying to play the role of the old wing forward in a 3:2:3 scrum, namely to lean on to the scrum in order to be quickly away when the ball has been lost so that they can tackle the outside half. I know I am repeating myself, but it must be clearly understood that this is useless under the present laws.

If you are a flanker in a 3:4:1 scrum you should pack down against the prop at the same time as the locks and apply your weight, leaving the No 8 forward the last to go down. It is now virtually impossible for you to catch the outside half, should your side lose the ball, and you should therefore be moving forward to pincer your opposition scrum half as in figure 28(a).

Even if you have lost the ball you must still apply your weight on the flanks of the scrum and resist the temptation to move backward behind the offside line (hindmost foot of the last man in the scrum) see figure 28(b).

If the scrum half runs instead of passing the ball, then you take him if he comes round your side of the scrum or, if one of the opposition loose forwards comes round the side of the scrum with the ball, take the first man; your own No 8 forward will take the second opponent round the scrum.

Now it may well be that you have been used to playing open or blind, left or right flanker – there is no need to change, provided you do change your running lines, that is, you are now primarily moving forward on to the opposition scrum half, and only if he has passed the ball do you move outwards in the direction of the outside half, assuming he is on your side of the field.

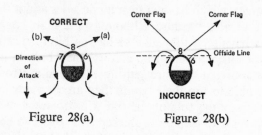

Figure 28(a)   Figure 28(b)

The role or shall we say running lines of the No 8 forward have also been slightly modified in recent years. Generally speaking on your own put-in the No 8 forward moves forward and follows the play; when it is the opposition put-in he normally moves backwards and to the opposite side to the ' put-in '.

In figure 28(a) therefore, in attack he would move forward to (b) side and in defence he would move backward to (a) side. He would also take the second man coming round the side of a scrum, as previously indicated. Quite obviously as he is now the last man down in the scrum he would have a good look round and decide in which direction the opposition would take the play, bearing in mind where the outside half is standing and the position on the field that the scrum is taking place. Not so long ago No 8 forwards used to take a straight line for the corner flag in defence (figure

28(b)), but this is not so apparent today as was seen from figure 28(a) and also when the overall defensive position of the forwards was looked at on page 88.

In a line-out, there is certain justification in saying that not much has changed in that the loose forwards can still arrange their defence so that one takes the scrum half at the back of the line-out, one moves towards the outside half and makes certain that he does not break back towards his own forwards and other, the No 8 forward, moves across the field and usually backwards. It is very common to use the hooker or blindside wing as the flanker at the front of the line-out.

Now it is very conceivable that the opposition will have a flanker whose job it is to get your scrum half round the back of the line-out. You would do well to remember that this flanker's job is made harder if you place yourself one position in the line-out in front of him so that he has to virtually run into you to get by.

Having established certain changes in role of the loose forwards, the need for co-ordination with their own half backs must be now stressed. All five must have a clear-cut division of labour; there must be no confusion; it is pointless to end up by saying 'I thought he was your man.' This link in defence is vital and really quite obvious, but the link does not end there, it must be apparent in the open field.

The loose forwards should be backing up on the inside of the outside half, the centres and the wings; they should also initiate their own attacking moves from scrums (for example, a No 8 pick up), line-outs (the peel) and short penalties.

There still remains one most important and fundamental difference between the roles of flankers and No 8 forward of today and those of yesteryear and this concerns their role as supporters of the loose ball. Flankers are invariably the first players to the breakdown point when a ball is dropped or a man in possession has been tackled and they should not 'seagull' or stand back and let the opposition get their hands on the ball, but aggressively contest possession themselves.

Admittedly a few wing forwards of a decade ago used to do this, but precious few. The ball is the most important thing and if it can be picked up and further movement made towards the opposition goal, then all well and good. If it is on the ground and cannot be picked up, then the first man there, probably one of the loose forwards, should put his foot over the man and ball.

The next two forwards up, regardless of their scrum position should bind tightly on to either side of this player to form what is in effect a platform or front row of a scrum. They must also keep on their feet or else the players arriving four and five will have nothing to drive on to. The three remaining forwards will complete the build-up of this scrum formation which is better and more accurately described as a ruck. (Reference pages 69-76.)

There is literally no substitute for being on the ball and being competitive at the same time, this is the hallmark of world-class loose forwards.

The Locks

When selectors are picking their locks they probably have a mental picture of the ideal player or pair of players, but, of course, selection is often a compromise. Similarly for the coach, his problem is to make the most of what he has got, so that each individual is encouraged to become a better player in every possible way.

Ideally, you would look for the clean, two-handed jumper, who combines this skill with tremendous strength, mobility and ball skill. In all he would be approximately 6ft 4½in and an athletic 16 stone.

It is quite obvious that few players combine these qualities, but that need not be a source of discouragement to any coach because if your forwards are incapable of getting the ball in the line-outs, then you adjust your tactics accordingly. First of all your team keep the ball on the island and not present the opposition with line-outs from which they can regain possession of the ball.

You can then vary the length of your line-out or throw the ball right over the top and take your chance at getting the ball from the ensuing chase. Do not give up – use your brains and adapt accordingly.

Getting back to our ideal lock or the player who you think could be that person with the necessary dedication, really strive for perfection in your charges – this is the only way you will help to make each and every one of them a better player. In passing, I have already indicated a number of qualities that locks should have and so let us look at their specific duties in a line-out and scrum.

Normally they are the team's jumpers (not always in schoolboy rugby) and as such would be advised to:

(a) Watch the ball at all times.
(b) Try and persuade the man marking him to jump before he does. This involves co-ordination between your jumper and the man throwing in the ball.
(c) Jump in front of your opposite number. For example: if he is standing at three, jump at two in line-out.
(d) Catch and control the ball with two hands (from one hand to two is acceptable).
(e) Turn as you are taking the ball so that you come down backing into opponents.
(f) Bring down the ball forcefully.
(g) Vary the time and position of the ball's delivery according to the wishes of the scrum half.

This is a slight expansion of the positional skill of line-out jumping you will find illustrated on pages 136-7.

I cannot resist commenting on the fairly recent line-out technique of indiscriminate flapping of the ball back to the poor unfortunate scrum half. For every time this works there always seems another occasion when the scrum half appears as a doormat for the opposition forwards. Only as a variant would I recommend this method, yet many teams seem to have adopted it as their standard line-out technique.

On the other hand, I am not averse to a ball being palmed, guided, steered or whatever you want to call it, to another part of the line-out before it is safely delivered to the scrum half – this makes sense. But flapping it straight back every time to the scrum half – no thank you, he is too precious a player to qualify for a posthumous award!

At first glance it appears that line-out work is simply a contest between respective jumpers from each team. Unfortunately, this is not the case, as has already been pointed out, for a combined forward effort plus the correct scrum half signal and accurate throw of the wing are vitally important if quality possession is to be obtained. The locks (jumpers) in the line-out need the assistance of every forward in their team, particularly the props, who normally wedge on to either side of the jumper.

Like the scrum, the line-out is an important platform or springboard from which attacks are launched and it helps enormously if that platform is moving forward when the ball leaves it; this will ensure that the opposition are either going backward or at worst remain stationary, as your own attack is launched. An aggressive jumper for the ball will ensure that the line-out does move forward.

Whereas the props help the locks in the line-out it is now the turn of the locks to help the props in the scrum (remember the part that flankers play as well?). Good scrumming depends on a number of factors, but being comfortable must be near the top of the list because if you are not comfortable then you can hardly be expected to apply your weight efficiently or have the maximum energy available for the open play.

Talk to your prop and get it sorted out. Sometimes the

position of your outside arm presents difficulty; experiment with these three grips on your prop.

Figure 29(a)   Figure 29(b)   Figure 29(c)

The position of a lock's feet in the scrum is always a bone of contention, especially if the scrum is having difficulty in holding a stationary position. In a 3:4:1 scrum the locks normally have their inside foot in front of their outside one, but certainly if the ball is to be channelled across the scrum then the feet positions are reversed.

However, I do not want to dwell on that point, but re-iterate the significance of the word lock itself and what it should mean to these players. Often you see a pack win the ball only to be pushed off it; this should not happen if the locks and No 8 are doing their job properly.

To ensure that you do not lose what you have worked so hard for, brace your knees, and with the inside of your feet firmly planted into the ground and behind you, retain this position. Naturally you should have your chin up so as to remove the camel-like hump which may have developed on your back.

A 'snap-shove' on the other hand stems from seven forwards (I exclude the hooker) straightening their legs in the scrum at the same time and also pulling with their hands and arms. This last point is very important as far as the

G

locks are concerned because they should be firmly gripping at the far junction of each other's shirt and shorts and pulling vigorously with their hands and arms as they straighten their legs. So often binding seems to mean dangling your arm over someone else's back!

In striving for the snap-shove it is obvious that a lock, who already has his legs straight before the ball comes in, can hardly be expected to push from this position – his knees must be bent prior to the ball coming in. If he finds difficulty in getting this position, and at the same time keeping a flat back, a useful tip to remember is to ask him to drop his knees towards the ground. This often improves the situation.

In the loose, lock forwards should naturally enough be everywhere the ball is, and if they can arrive at the rucks bound together, then their combined drive will have a tremendous impact. Purely as a guide to their ' running lines ' they would tend to move in the direction of the goal posts in both attack and defence (illustrated in figures 19 and 25).

The Props

The importance of scrumming your opponents into the ground has long been accepted by coaches as being a fairly sure way of ending the last fifteen minutes of the game well on top of the opposition. South Africa more than any other country has revelled in this strategy and as the results table shows at the beginning of this book, it has been mighty successful.

The pillars of any scrum are your two props; if they are weak and easily bent or split from their hooker then your whole scrum slowly but surely disintegrates.

Ideally, a lock forward would push on a barn-door of a man and this is repeatedly what South African props have been like over the years. They have consistently produced 6ft props of 16 or 17 stone who have been absolutely immovable.

However, the last few years has produced a new element in world class prop forward play and that is mobility.

New Zealand has produced a number of props who have been able to combine these immovable qualities with sufficient mobility to trip merrily round the field like loose forwards. Perhaps it was an accident at first (knowing the New Zealand approach this seems doubtful) but the word got round that if you wanted to prop for the All Blacks then the 16 or 17 stone that you were carrying would have to be moved from scrum to ruck, from line-out to ruck at a speed greater than anything seen before, or else you just would not get a look in.

Such a change in the accepted role of a prop has had an even more beneficial effect on New Zealand forward play and the sight of these eight huge men moving round the paddock reminded one rugby writer of the ' Derby field coming round Tattenham Corner '. Not the sort of description a team playing New Zealand would want to hear in the dressing room before stepping out to face them.

Moving back to more earthly creatures there are a few points to note when selecting your props. Often long-backed props or players with a weak dorsal region have difficulty in keeping their back flat and unless they have exceptional strength they may well be advised to try another position.

Usually you play your heavier prop on the tight head side in order to give the scrum some balance and also to counter the tendency for the scrum to swing. If you have watched scrums which accidentally swing or are deliberately wheeled you will notice that the natural way for them to move is towards the loose head side. A very heavy and solid tight head could in part counter this action.

The principal function of a prop in the scrum is to support his hooker and be in a position to transmit the weight of the scrum onto the opposing props (3:4:1 scrum). If he can do this then the important job of winning your own put-in will be made much easier.

The position of the prop's arms is important. Normally with his inside arm he would try to grasp the far junction of the hooker's shirt and shorts and in the case of the loose head prop of the team putting in the ball his outside arm has to be on the inside of that of the near prop of the opposing team.

If your scrum half is putting the ball into the scrum it is usual for the props to have their outside foot in front of the inside foot. This is particularly important on the loose head side because the ball is deflected by the hooker through his loose head's prop's feet (see page 149).

Not so very long ago the loose head prop used to follow the ball into the scrum and trap it with the hooker's foot. Some still do this, but it has lost favour because inevitably the prop was perched on one foot (his inside one) to do this and consequently it made it very difficult for the left lock to stop himself slipping through into the front row, with a consequent loss in forward drive to the scrum.

When it is the opposition put-in, then the tight head has an important part to play if the hooker is going to take the ball against the head. The tight head must, by using his outside foot help the hooker to trap and drag the ball back. You can also increase your chance of winning a tight head ball by deliberately wheeling the scrum in that direction.

As we have seen when discussing the locks, the props have a very important job to do in the line-outs. They must wedge in on either side of the jumper. Although two methods of doing this are advocated on page 136, the following should also be stressed at this stage. Make certain that you wedge in on the jumper at the correct time. That is, *not until the ball has been touched by the jumper*; you can then drive the jumper forward.

A prop is very much concerned with supporting the ball in the loose and too much emphasis cannot be given to working out some signal between scrum half and forwards so as to indicate the direction the play is going whether the ball has been won or lost.

The props will probably be last away from scrums (this is not always true) and if you expect them to get to the breakdown point you must give them some indication of where the ball is, otherwise they will pick their heads up, look around and only then move off. This is a needless waste of time.

As I have mentioned before, this signal would, on your own put-in preferably come before the ball has actually been put into the scrum so that the props can be attuning themselves to the next situation.

Do not forget that as life gets more sedentary, props in particular must possess sufficient physical strength to carry out their job and therefore the coach would be well advised to see that weight training (Chapter Thirteen) is an integral part of the long term preparation for these players.

The Hooker

Ask any hooker the score at the end of the game and he won't give you the result of the match, but something like three to one, or five to two. He is referring to the private match that has taken place between himself and his opposite number and these scores represent the number of times he won the ball against the head and the number of times he lost his own put-in.

In the above examples he would be telling you that he had won three and five balls against the head and lost one and two respectively. Whilst winning the ball in the scrum is obviously of the utmost importance, the over-riding question remains, 'were they quality possession?'

There is no doubt that often winning the ball on the opposition put-in works wonders for morale and more in particular presents the team winning the ball with a wonderful opportunity of attacking whilst their opponents are lying steep in anticipation of winning their own put-in. However, hookers who are only interested in this private duel are too inward looking and perhaps neglecting many other aspects of forward play.

There is no doubt that hooking is a highly specialized skill, and it is quite remarkable how hookers seem to mature like wine; the older they get, the better they become, which is testimony to the tremendous importance that must be attached to experience.

You cannot learn the latter, you acquire it by diligent application of the techniques of hooking over a long period of time. Many sides are quite prepared to carry a man if he is an accomplished hooker, but it is obviously most desirable to have someone who can also play a major role in general play.

Moving to the actual technique of hooking one can say immediately that if the snap-shove of the pack is such that the hooker finds his foot over the ball as soon as it comes into the tunnel, then it is an incredibly simple business.

Unfortunately few hookers experience playing with such a scrum and usually they have to work hard for their own put-in. The following points are therefore important.

(i)   The hooker *must* be able to see the ball and there-fore, the loose head prop should be higher than the tight head prop on the hooker's own put-in.

A hooker relies very much on the support of his props, which is probably why many people say that ' a hooker is as good as his props '.

(ii) On his own put-in the hooker is advised to use his far foot because he is able to control the ball more easily. Note – he can deflect the ball with his near foot if he prefers, but it is not such a strong posi-tion.

(iii) Merely to get possession of the ball is not enough – by varying the angle of his strike he can vary the path of the ball, and, therefore, where it can be picked up by his scrum half. He should strive for this degree of perfection.

(iv)   Quality possession is dependent on the weight of the scrum being applied at the correct time, and also on how the scrum half puts the ball into the scrum.

Remember the scrum half should stand one yard away. So many of them creep much closer than this with the result that the ball is no sooner in the scrum than it is bouncing madly out at the back. This is bad ball, and the scrum half is generally clobbered by his opposite number as soon as he tries to pick it up.

Only by standing the correct distance from the scrum, by holding the ball at the correct angle for the put-in and constantly practising with the whole forward unit will this and other faults be eradicated.

(v)   Striking against the head. Method One: The hooker uses the outside of his near foot. Remember that the tight head helps to 'trap' the ball by using his outside foot. Method Two: The hooker turns his face in the direction of his loose head and then looks down and to the tight head side so he knows when to strike with the inside of his near foot. Both these methods are illustrated under Individual Skills (page 149).

(vi)   There are three accepted ways of binding. One arm over each of your prop's shoulders is used on your own put-in and usually allows you a fairly tight bind, which is particularly important in this case. One arm under each of your prop's shoulders is not very satisfactory because this method tends to put you further away from where the ball will pitch in the tunnel. Finally one arm under and one arm over your prop's shoulder is best used when you are striking against the head because it allows you just that little bit more movement of the body which is necessary if you are to reach the ball.

(vii) Feet positions – these are principally governed by the Laws of the Game, although you would obviously want them forward rather than right back and your weight would be principally taken on the non-striking foot. For the schoolmaster coach, you would be well advised to look for boys with long, strong arms for binding, a short back and longish supple legs for striking. He obviously must have quick reactions and boys who have played soccer or who are good dribblers of the ball often turn out to be more than useful hookers. Look for the wag, the boy who has plenty to say for himself, he also often has the wits to be a hooker.

Turning from the hooker in a scrum to the forward at the front of the line-out, it would be appropriate to say that much is expected of him these days. So often he is used as a flanker at the front of the line-out, whose job it is to catch and dispossess the opposition scrum half when the ball has been lost.

No one should come round the front of the line-out inside the five yard area – this is his territory. The hooker who can read the game and has ball handling skill can plague the life of the opposition down the blind side of the field and also because he tends to move down the centre of the field to follow up attacks, he is in a wonderful position to take cross kicks and harry the opposition full back.

As with so many positions over the field, not sufficient is demanded of this player, and therefore, his latent talent often goes unused.

1. Here is a demonstration of an unusual, yet effective way of screening the ball. Note how the ball carrier is driving into an opponent with his shoulder. The receiver of the ball is well positioned to keep the ball *moving forward*. (Cross the GAIN LINE – key factor No 4)

2. They say every picture tells a story and Colin Mead's story is that if you run at the 'correct angle' and 'drive forward' *not* only will you take a lot of stopping (five Englishmen are committed), but you will almost certainly find yourself in a position to create a ruck when you are finally checked

3. 'Willie John' McBride of Ireland shows a powerful position from which to feed the ball to his scrum-half (having just caught the ball in the line-out with two hands and backed into the position). Note how wide his base of support is and how far the ball is from the opposition (England)

4. Albie Bates, Tommy Bedford and Piet Greyling (*L to R*) of South Africa show the determination and compactness that you would expect to see in top class loose forwards as they leave the line-out in pursuit of the opposition halfbacks. Nigel Starmer-Smith (England) is one jump (or dive) ahead of them on this occasion

5. Rod Webb of England, one of many outstanding English wings, demonstrates a key coaching point, 'Carry the ball in two hands'

6. A neat pivot-pass by Dawie de Villiers clears the ball from a South
African scrum against England (1970). Which arm would you go for if
you were trying to spoil this pass? See how Roger Shackleton (outside
half) is driving hard for his opposite number – more important than
ever these days

7. John Spencer (Cambridge University) is well positioned to take a
'flat pass' from Gerald Davies (Cambridge University) if the latter
draws John Carroll the Oxford University fullback (black shirted
player nearest white line)

8. *Above*: *Two-handed catch* and *turn* by Frik de Preez of South Africa. All eyes on the ball – Every forward in the line-out is a potential gatherer of the ball. Key coaching points. 9. *Below*: Two great Australian halfbacks Phil Hawthorne and Ken Catchpole demonstrate the importance of always making the ball available (Hawthorne is doing it) even when tackled. Catchpole shows superb positional skill, and after taking this pass, goes on to score a try against England in January 1967

10

Backs as a Unit

The object of the game as we have discovered in Chapter Five is to finish up at the end of eighty minutes having scored more points than your opponents and in this aim the backs should play a major role. Their object or aim therefore is to score tries; points acquired through kicks may be termed a bonus and in attempting to score tries the backs obviously must be attack conscious.

However, it is rather a pointless exercise to score tries, only to discover that you are letting the opposition do exactly the same through your inept defence.

It is, therefore, at defence that I shall look first because an organized and positive defence will give you the necessary confidence to devote as much time as possible to attack.

This sort of defence will involve you in having a thorough understanding of the *gain and tackle line* and you would do well to refresh yourself by glancing at pages 35-41 again. Obviously if you can stop the opposition from crossing the gain line you are more than half way to starting a counter attack.

The backs therefore must come up together just on the inside of their opposite numbers and try to take man and ball. They won't always be successful, but if they are mentally tuned to not only stopping their opposite number, but getting the ball off him as well, then their tackling will be really effective.

The strengths and weaknesses of your own back line as well as that of the opposition must be noted. If your outside half is not coming up in defence, or a centre is too slow and continually being beaten by his opposite number, or getting in front of his own outside half, thus leaving a potential gap, somebody has to do something about it. Talk to each other, encourage each other and work to cover each other's mistakes.

Remember your alignment in both attack and defence is rather like a gate closing. It must be orderly, positive and progressive, in that you take your cue from the player on your inside. If the opposition introduce an extra man in the line then move in one and take the man with the ball; this should leave your full back wtih only one opponent to stop.

It is courting disaster to allow the extra man to run whilst you shadow your opposite number, particularly if the extra man has appeared in the back-line outside his own outside half or between his centres.

Even if the extra man in the line is only acting as a link it is quite staggering how many times the final pass is knocked on or thrown forward as a result of the pressure to which the quick defenders subject the attackers.

This method of countering the extra man in the line holds good for scrums and line-outs. It is also vital that defence is properly organized to receive kick-offs, twenty-five drop outs, short penalties and kicks at goal. From rucks and mauls, defence is very much harder because almost certainly you will be on the retreat and possibly have a fellow back trapped under the ruck or caught in the maul.

You must be even quicker up on the opposition in these circumstances and anticipate that they will attack down your most vulnerable flank – this will probably be down your blind or short side of the field.

The following figures, 30, 31, 32 should illustrate your approximate positions more accurately than words can.

The full back, 15, takes one side of the field and the blind side wing (11 in this case) or the scrum half takes the other. If the ball is dropped out to your forwards then you should move back to your normal alignment (see figures 30, 31).

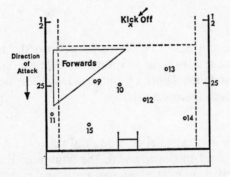

Figure 30

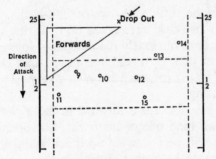

Figure 31

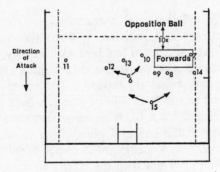

Figure 32

Short Penalty

Whilst the positional emphasis here is on the backs, the role of the loose forwards is vital to the defence. Usually the forwards watch the short or blind side of the field whilst the backs watch the open side.

Kick at Goal

Whether a kick at goal is successful or not, there should be little problem in dealing with the situation. However, if the kick strikes a post then the resultant ricochet could prove dangerous unless speedily dealt with. If the kick at goal is from quite a long way out then the ricochet from the post could be dealt with by the half-backs.

However, if the kick were taken on or inside the twenty-five yard area then obviously the defending forwards would be much nearer their own goal line and at least one of them should be delegated to watch his own goal posts for such a ricochet occurring.

It is more practical for a forward in these circumstances to take the ball than one of his backs, because the opposition forwards will be following up quickly and it would be silly for a back to be caught under a ruck or in an ensuing maul and thereby leave a gap in the defence.

From a really efficient and workmanlike defence those backs with courage and initiative will see the opportunity for counter-attack. If a team has been continually pounding your defence, there is every chance that a quick and incisive counter-attack will bring its rewards. The game of soccer provides a good example of what I mean, where sides who have packed their defence for minutes on end have suddenly won or intercepted the ball and raced away to score at the other end. If every man is engaged in attack then there is no one to defend and players with the ability to read the game will not let such situations go begging.

I have already said that the full back has a vital role in this respect, but for him to counter-attack with confidence, he needs instant support from the rest of his backs. They must not stand still and let the full back catch them up – they must move back and help; particularly is this true of the wings. How many coaches incorporate counter-attack under sustained and continuous pressure in their team practice sessions?

Unfortunately very few and yet this is one of the best ways of playing against teams with a rigid and well-rehearsed pattern or system of play. Let me repeat, the full back is the key. If he cannot run and beat oncoming flankers then you are only left with virtually two alternatives. You try to kick and roll the ball into touch or you play ' aerial ping-pong ' with the other full back.

In both instances you are giving the opposition a needless opportunity of getting the ball back again.

As we move to attacking play in its more generally accepted form, that is from scrums and line-outs, apart from understanding all the key factors (Chapter Five), a few additional points need to be stressed.

The ball is the property of the team and no individual player should monopolize it or misuse it by dying with it. Rugby is a team game and it is everyone's responsibility to support the ball and a team mate, so that if a back is tackled the nearest man picks up the ball and moves it on towards the opposition goal line. The nearest man will often be a fellow back.

Even though it looks certain that someone on your side is going to score, support him until he in fact does so. Similarly, always chase kicks ahead. Probably ninety-nine times out of a hundred it will be a waste of time, but you can bet a pound to a penny that the one occasion you fail to follow up, a try was yours for the begging.

I have already stressed that it is a team game and that the backs more than anyone should understand the need for playing the game in front of their forwards. I've outlined that you can cross the gain line by outflanking your opponents or by penetrating their back line. I've also pointed out on page 38 that you can cross the gain line by kicking; I've also spelt out the dangers of kicking.

On page 39 figure 5 shows the areas in which you would be advised to kick and also the sort of kick to use. All of this is important knowledge to have, but it is useless knowledge unless it is turned into a practical reality through diligent practice as a unit and as a team.

During a game the back unit should be striving to stretch the opposition until they are either fatigued or out of position. To do this obviously you want quality possession, but at the same time you must present your opponents with problems created through your own skill and quick wits.

The moves illustrated in figure 33 have proved popular, and more important, successful, over the past three seasons. However, the fact that they are now well known will make them much more difficult to repeat and therefore you would be well advised to look at them from one standpoint only; that standpoint being, 'in what way did they create problems for the defending side?' If you can discover that, then maybe you can develop your own moves.

Other attacking situations occur from your own kick off, twenty-five yard drop and short penalty, if you have taken the time to practise them. Apart from having thoroughly rehearsed any short penalty move, the scrum half (usually) must get the ball in his hands immediately the penalty has been awarded; speed on moving the ball is vital if you hope to catch the opposition unawares.

To round off this section I would commend every player (backs in this instance) and coach, to have a thorough knowledge of the key factors and to remember that the ball that has been so difficult to win belongs to the whole team and not to any one individual.

The onus, therefore, is on each back to make the most of every situation and make certain that the ball never dies, but is continually being moved forward towards the opposition goal line. This is the continuity aspect required.

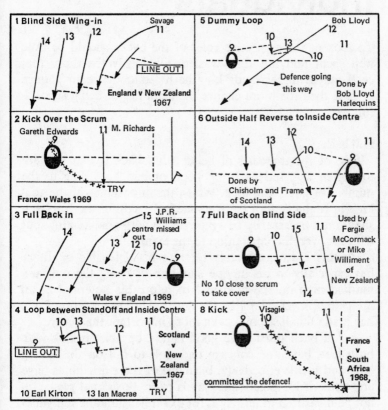

Figure 33

11

Backs as Individuals

To look at the respective roles of the backs should be time well spent and not time wasted. Obviously the more that each player understands how he fits into the team pattern of play then the more chance the team has of being successful.

Full back

One of the tragedies of being a full back is that you are too often assessed as being good or bad according to the number of goals you kick. Whilst the importance of the goal kick in rugby cannot be overstated, the skill of the full back should not necessarily be synonymous with goal-kicking, but with his overall contribution to the team.

By this I do not merely refer to his defensive qualities, but especially to his unique situation of being the only un-marked man on the field and therefore his potential as an attacking player. Happily, the Australian Dispensation Law, has made this last point even more important than ever.

A full back must have good hands, be able to kick with both feet, have the courage and skill to fall on the rolling ball, and tackle effectively, but none of these attributes have any value if his positional play is poor. Positional play cannot be measured in terms of, for example, standing ten yards behind the threequarter backs, but by whether or not the full back allows the ball to bounce.

The good full back is under everything and at the same time in a position to clear his line immediately or start a counter-attack. Also, if his positional play is sound then rarely will he find himself confronted by an opponent who has the choice of beating him either way. He will have so positioned himself that the opponent can only go one way; usually towards the touchline.

Rightly, in my opinion, I have stressed the importance of positional play and the two simple ways of checking whether a full back has this skill, are (a) does he let the ball bounce, and (b) is he often caught flat-footed?

How do you help yourself to cultivate the skill of correct positioning? Anticipation! In the first place you watch the opposition outside half and try to read the signal he gives to his scrum half. It's generally a very simple signal like a hand on the left or right thigh. When it is a scrum you must also make certain that the scrum half has not arranged a move with his No 8 forward and/or flankers.

Sometimes he taps them on the back to indicate that they will be involved in a move when the ball has been won. For example, if the French wanted to cancel their outside half's directional signal and try a move involving the loose forwards, their scrum half used to simply give a thumbs down and the outside half knew that he wasn't getting the ball.

Another point to note is the direction in which the scrum half is facing when he puts the ball into the scrum. Shall we say seven times out of ten the scrum half would pass to his outside half's right because this would not involve the scrum half in turning to pass when he picked the ball up at the base of the scrum. There is also less chance of the opposition scrum half catching him as he passes the ball.

From line-outs the direction in which the opposition attack is going to move is even more obvious, especially as most teams play an orthodox line-out close to the five yard line. However, as we have seen, if they were to take the whole line-out another ten yards into the field of play this would give them two sides to attack instead of the present one. Still as a full back you don't want to give the opposition ideas and make your own job harder.

For a scrum in a central position you would be standing

H

more or less straight behind the scrum ready to move to either side; if the scrum were nearer the touchlines or if it were a line-out then you would tend to take up a position behind and slightly to the open side of your own outside half so that as the ball was moved by your opponents you would be just on the inside of the opposition back who had the ball.

By doing this you should be able to stop any break that might occur and be on the inside of the wing threequarter should the latter get the ball and round his opposite number. With experience you will discover how to run him towards the touchline.

Beware of standing in a position to take a pass directly from your scrum half on or near your own goal line. If the opposition win the ball against the head or if it is their own put-in you will have to be desperately fast to cover an orthodox handling movement by the opposition backs and especially if they add an extra man to their back line.

Again you should be standing behind and just outside your own outside half if it is a line-out or a scrum near a touchline; or if it is a scrum in a more central position than normally you would guard one side of the field and your outside half the other.

I should be inclined to encourage the half backs to get rid of the ball in such defensive situations rather than the scrum half passing the ball back to you. Finally, try to avoid standing in your own goal area; come up to the goal line. A mistake in your own goal area is usually fatal.

In general play I have stressed the need for never being caught flat-footed so that your opponent can take his choice as to which side he beats you on. However, there will inevitably be occasions when you are faced by one or two men, but do not worry, there are one or two things that you can do to help yourself. First of all, never take a dummy, always take the man with the ball; this is the golden rule.

Whether you are faced with one or two men, move to the

man with the ball at a controlled speed, so that you shorten
the distance between yourselves and consequently make him
think and react much quicker. Sometimes you can panic him
into getting rid of the ball before he has really committed
you and consequently you could then be left with a one
versus one situation. By your moving to the man with the
ball, he might find that he hasn't time to get rid of the ball
and so tackling him is made easy for you.

Sometimes, when you get the situation as in figure 35
(page 130) you can make the man with the ball think that
you are not going to tackle him, by moving ever so slightly
towards the outside opponent, who in this case is a winger.
The man with the ball thinks he can dummy you and finds
that he has misread the situation.

Let us now look at the attacking potential of the full
back. A full back can join the attack after the ball has been
won in a ruck or maul, line-out and scrum, simply by moving up from his position and joining the back line. There is
always danger in doing this, but with constant practice the
advantages far outweigh the disadvantages. Your ultimate
skill in being able to exploit the technique of coming into
the back line is to recognize when you can (a) penetrate the
oppositon, (b) act as a link.

Where a full back enters the line is immaterial, the timing
of his entry is the important point and again this depends
on unit practice. If by entering the back line he is to penetrate the opposition, then he must take the ball on the burst,
so that as the two sets of backs meet he is through them
before the opposition realize it. His starting position is important – he does not want to telegraph the opposition of his
intentions. At the same time he does not want to move so
late that he cannot catch up with his own backs.

A good guide is to move up into the attack as the ball
is delivered to your own scrum half. From scrums and line-
outs you would always tell the backs in front of you when
and where you were coming into the attack. Normally you

would join the attack on the open side of the field, but quite often you are just as dangerous to the opposition by entering the attack on the blind or short side of the field.

Someone must cover you and therefore you would tell the appropriate winger, a simple signal will often suffice, but remember, from a scrum or line-out, those in front of you must know what you are doing. From rucks and mauls it is virtually impossible to give adequate warning and the backs in front of you must therefore anticipate your intentions.

These last points obviously still hold good if you come into the back line to act as a link or extra pair of hands. In this case you would almost certainly have to draw-an-opponent in order to create the overlap for your winger. This will be one of the first individual skills we will look at in Chapter Twelve.

A full back can also contribute enormously by way of counter-attack, particularly when the opposition have missed touch or a kick at goal. Usually he is confronted by one or two players rushing up to harass him and if he can dummy or sidestep, then he normally has twenty to thirty yards of clear space in which to develop a counter-attack. However, only if he gets support from the rest of the backs can he do this with any real confidence.

Therefore, the team must get into the habit of coming back to help rather than just stand waiting for the full back to reach them. In any team game you try and make your opponents misread your intentions and for a full back to counter-attack he would be well advised to take note of this point. It is illustrated as follows.

If as a full back, you catch a badly placed kick from your opponents and one or two of them think you are going to kick to touch, even if you have caught the ball outside your own twenty-five yard area, this will almost certainly make them slow down and try to charge down your kick. Now that you have got them thinking you are putting the ball into touch, you produce your sidestep and off you go counter-attacking. Of course, I have made it sound very easy and it is, after hours of practice!

If on the other hand you catch the same badly placed kick from your opponents, put your head back and start running, then the chase is really on. That is not to say you won't be successful in starting a counter attack, but your intentions are obvious.

Finally, I would just mention the importance of being able to kick with either foot from any position. A one-footed full back is soon found out and in a tight game where he may be under pressure, any weakness in this department of his game is often ruthlessly exposed. If you can screw kick (page 146) then you would use your left foot for kicking into a touch line on the right hand side of the field and vice-versa. This sort of kick with the correct foot can often add twenty or thirty yards on to a kicker's length.

Do not be fooled by the kicker who thumps the ball a prodigious height and largely into the crowd. The effective kick is the one which not only gets the distance, but only pitches one yard over the touch line – none of the kick is then wasted. There is little doubt that the full back with these skills at his finger tips, plus initiative and flair can completely alter the whole character of a game.

Wing Backs

To see a wing in full cry for the line is one of the many pleasures of rugby football, unless, of course, you are the player who is marking him. Unfortunately wingers have been looked upon for far too long as fringe players with just this one function. The scoring of tries is, of course, their most important duty and in order to do this a winger should have physical speed, and more important, speed of thought. Being in the right place at the right time is not often an accident.

As with many of the individual roles, the demands that are now made upon the winger have considerably increased over the years. If a wing only gets two or three passes of the ball during the course of a game these days, then he simply cannot be looking for work, and look for work he most certainly must do. There is no reason why he should not be the original source of penetration rather than the finisher off of moves.

Many sides are now using the blind side winger as an extra full back or as an extra attacker by constantly bringing him into the back line from his blind side position. The past season has even seen one county list their team as having a right and left full back and play them in these positions.

At least it does show that coaches and captains are endeavouring to find ways of using the player who usually has more speed than anyone else on the team.

The ability to swerve, sidestep or to have a change of pace are most useful skills for the winger to have if he is going to enhance his scoring chances, but as with tackling, these attributes are of little help if he cannot position himself correctly to use them. Positioning must be based on the player's knowledge of his own capabilities and those of his opponent(s).

Thus, for example, the slower physically strong wing would be ill-advised to attempt to outpace his opponent to the line without having first committed his man by running at him, in order to either (a) catch him flat-footed so that he can either step inside or outside him, or (b) hand him off, (c) shoulder charge him off or (d) screen pass to put a supporting player clear, etc.

Wingers of real class are few and far between but they are easily recognized by their balanced running and their ability to create and take chances which would not be possible for lesser mortals. All good players carry the ball in two hands because only when you do this can you effectively distribute it in the event of say, a tackle. (See Plate 5.) However, there will be occasions when it is necessary to carry the ball under one arm, for example to hand off an opponent, in which case you would transfer the ball from two hands to the hand farthest away from your opponent. This is a common failing of inexperienced players in that they either put the ball under the wrong arm or telegraph their intentions by putting the ball under an arm far too early.

If you are in the habit of tucking the ball under an arm it is fairly obvious to an opponent that you cannot pass it and therefore he knows who to tackle. The vital factor in the art of handing off an opponent is timing. If you can find your opponent's head as he commits himself to the tackle then it is generally possible to push yourself further away from his outstretched arms, for failure to effect the hand-off will, as I have just pointed out, make distribution of the ball very difficult.

Ideally the ball should not die in the hands of any player and in this respect a winger is no exception for he should in the last resort seek to create a ruck, or cross kick, rather than allow himself to be bundled into touch.

In defence the good blind side winger will always see-saw with the full back when the latter is attacking. He should consider this as part of his normal duties and if it fits in with the team strategy then he can also prove a most effective flank forward at the front of the line-out.

I have deliberately left the vexed question of throwing the ball into the line-out to the last. If the winger is entrusted with this vitally important duty, and there is no reason why he should be, he must remember to keep the ball in the view of the catcher at all times and be able to throw with extreme accuracy in all weather conditions, or else you can forget about winning your own ball from the line-outs.

How many wingers own their own rugby ball so that they can practise every day of the week? Although the fairly recent Dispensation Law has reduced the number of line-outs in a match, the reduction is not so marked that this skill is not still of the highest importance.

From what has been said it is evident that the winger must strive to be the complete footballer with the ability to seize half chances with unfailing tenacity.

Centre Backs

A centre, by the very nature of his position, is a penetrator first and foremost, but he is also required to feed his wing, and tackle in such a way as to turn defence into attack, that is, take man and ball. Some centres prefer to play left and right or inside and outside, but rarely do centres of the same style go together and if you consider such well known pairings as Jackie Matthews and Bleddyn Williams; Phil Davies and Jeff Butterfield; Mickey Weston and Malcolm Phillips; and David Duckham and John Spencer, you will see that one of the pair has genuine speed, sidestep and swerve, and the other has strength, a devastating tackle and/or the ability to distribute the ball well.

Between them, therefore, are the necessary ingredients to outwit the opposition, yet generally only one of them has caught the imagination of the public.

As a general rule the centre with the sidestep and swerve is played as the outside centre and the devastating tackler and good distributor of the ball is on the inside. So many centres make the mistake of trying to make a break every time; or running across the field and then passing the ball; of kicking as soon as the ball is in their hands; of standing so far apart that as soon as backline moves, the link between each other is lost; of not supporting the ball after it has been passed, etc.

Everyone must be prepared to learn from their mistakes and centres are no exception. They must study the methods of better players, particularly their opponents and profit from playing against players who are better than themselves. You can learn more in one afternoon from playing against someone who is better than you are, with a subsequent chat in the evening, than all the reading or coaching in the world.

Although it may not always be wise to attempt a break the good centre will never miss the opportunity to do so, by, for example, using the sidestep, swerve, shoulder charge, or hand-off, in other words the individual skills. In the event of there being no possibility of making a break the worst thing a centre can do is to dither, he must be prepared to take positive action in helping other members of his side to score.

He can do this by (a) creating a gap; perhaps attempting to draw his co-centre's opposite number by going for the gap between the opposition centres. This is often known as making the half break; (b) acting as a link; by feeding the ball at great speed to the wing (generally with the blindside wing or full back in the line) so as to outflank the opposition.

Perhaps only experience will tell you which of the above you should apply for any given situation, but constant unit and team practice related to your observations of the capabilities of the opposition will help you to decide just that split second quicker the correct course of action. If the opposition have attacked down their blindside of the field you must be prepared to turn back and cover quickly, but you must always return to your normal alignment for a scrum or line-out as quickly as possible.

Finally, for the coach, it is so important to remind the centres of where the try line is. This may seem ridiculously obvious, but if it encourages them to run hard and straight and if their practice sessions are geared to this end, then much will have been achieved because as has already been pointed out in Chapter Five, little progress was ever made in the direction of the side lines.

Half Back Unit—Scrum Half and Outside Half

To the old, yet true, maxim that *forwards win matches* one could add with safety, that the forwards will win their matches much easier if they are nursed along by good half backs. Although the scrum and outside half are individuals, any success that they acquire as a partnership is the keystone of team success in attack.

Collectively they are the main distributors of the ball, but in particular, they are in a position to mould the pattern of play. It therefore follows that the half backs must practise with each other at all times so that they completely understand each other's signals and can transmit them to the rest of the backs, as well as to the forwards.

The last point perhaps needs a word of explanation. By talking to each other it should be quite simple for each member of the back division to know precisely what is on. It should also be possible for the scrum half to transmit any signal from his outside half to the forwards at scrums and line-outs, so that they (the forwards) will know in which direction the play will go after the ball has been won by them. They can then move in the correct direction and support in strength.

In an effort to play the ball in front of their forwards the half backs must unbalance the opposition loose forwards (two flankers and No 8) and half backs. The necessary doubt can in part be created in the minds of the opposition by varying the angle and distance at which the half backs stand in relation to each other. If uncertainty can be created in the minds of the loose forwards and opposition half backs then it should be possible for the outside half to take a flat pass and really accelerate over the gain line. They must also link in both attack and defence with their own loose forwards.

Recent law changes make it vital for the half backs to tackle their opposite numbers; particularly is this true of the outside half from a scrum, because flank forwards are much more tied down than they used to be. The half backs can help to give the game its aimed for continuity by linking with the threequarter backs and their own loose forwards. They must be decisive in all they do, try to cross the gain line by varying their tactics, deal effectively with bad ball and conserve the energy of their forwards.

Half backs should be wide awake to the possibilities of moving the ball from a tight head heel and from an opposition throw-in at a line-out – even in their own twenty-five yard area. Remember in these circumstances the opposition backs will probably be aligned in an attacking position and not prepared for this quick and incisive attack. All of these things can only be achieved in a match after vigilant team practice.

Having merely glanced at the enormous task that the half backs are called upon to perform as a partnership, one can look at their individual requirements at this point and start by saying that they must be players of high natural ability.

Scrum Half

In athletics a very accurate somato typing of the Olympic Gold Medallists has taken place and now that the physical requirements needed to be an 800 metre champion as opposed to a 5,000 metres are well known, athletes can to a certain extent be channelled into the activity which affords them the greater opportunities of meeting with success.

There has been no parallel study of rugby players, as far as I know, but if you were asked to describe the physical requirements of a top class scrum half you would probably say; between 5ft 6in and 5ft 8in, ten and twelve stone, quick reactions, decisive in his judgement and physically resilient. You then tack on the ability to pass accurately, kick with either foot, tackle, fall on the ball and cover.

These points are all very important, but no more so than for any other player on the field and therefore we must look at his positional play for further guidance. If you are physically unfit then you cannot hope to display any of the individual skill that you may possess and similarly if your knowledge of positional play is bad this is also bound to affect your play.

Duties of a Scrum Half at a scrum

    (i)   You receive your outside half's signal.

   (ii)   You check your position on the field (e.g. your own twenty-five – their half, etc) and see if a move with the No 8 or flank forwards is called for.

  (iii)   If it is, let your outside half know.

  (iv)   Whether it is or not, you must give your forwards some directional signal, so that after the ball has been won they know in which direction to support.

   (v)   You stand one yard from the scrum, ball held in two hands midway between knee and ankle, and in one forward movement in goes the ball.

  (vi)   Remember it is easier to pass in the same direction as you have put the ball in, but your outside half may already have indicated that he wants to go the other way so what do you do? (a) You can put the ball in the scrum and move immediately to the rear of the scrum to wait for it. The ball will have to be channelled to the No 8's feet or the far side of the scrum, otherwise you will not have the time to take up this position. If the channelling has taken place then you can pass either to the left or the right with ease. (b) If it has not been done, but comes out of the nearside of the scrum then you may have to reverse pass.

       These sort of problems are, in part, why it is easier for a scrum half to pass in the same direction that he puts the ball into the scrum.

  (vii)   Assuming your scrum has lost the ball against the head and you are following your opposite number round the scrum. Call to your own forwards 'Ball lost', 'Ball being held', then 'Ball gone right or left' when the opposition scrum half passes or runs.

 (viii)   If you are trying to catch your opposite number,

keep behind the ball and when he gets his hands on it don't go for his legs, but for one of his arms. All you have to do is knock one of them and you have ruined his pass and at the same time probably put your team into an attacking position. (See Plate 6.)

At a Line-out

(i) If you are giving the signals make certain that the forwards and the man throwing in the ball see them and also that you indicate the direction the play will go when you have won the ball.

(ii) Do not leave an excessive gap between yourself and the line-out.

(iii) Avoid turning your back on the opposition when giving your outside half a pass. Why? If you turn you will lose sight of the opposition loose forwards and therefore they could intercept your pass or arrive ready to tackle your outside half at the same time that he receives your pass.

(iv) Try to keep your feet when passing – a man on the ground is a man out of the game.

(v) The direction that a scrum half takes when he and his team have lost possession will to some extent depend on the overall defensive system, but usually, in simple terms, a scrum half covers his full back. Obviously he would move to any ruck or maul which developed en route.

Rucks and Mauls

Only three points of real importance need be said.

(i) Always be on the heels of the forwards in rucks and mauls. The ball, when it does appear, is yours and yours alone, unless of course you are under the ruck and someone else has taken your place.

(ii) The ball must be moved quickly. The scrum half must not allow himself to be caught.

(iii) The scrum half must be exploring the possibilities of using the short side of the field. I do not mean he half-heartedly tries to use it when he gets the ball, but he should have made a mental picture, before the ball has appeared from a ruck or a maul, as to whether or not the blind side is guarded. Upon getting the ball he does not hesitate; he goes himself, uses his outside half down this side of the field, his full back and/or his blind side wing. Why? From the original scrum it is obvious where the opposition backs would be lying and therefore to move the ball in the same direction from the ensuing ruck would be to run into the opposition backs again.

If you use the blind side, however, you would most likely have only the opposition blind side wing and full back to contend with and if your own full back comes up into the attack then a try should be yours for the begging. Remember, you can over-use the short or blind side of the field – keep your eyes open and note where the opposition are weakest or thinnest in terms of numbers. Use the space, scan with your eyes and switch the direction of the attack.

Outside Half

The outside half has marvellous hands, is nimble of foot and is the master of all situations, or so he should be. You might say he is dependent on his scrum half for quality possession, but the scrum half in turn is very much dependent on his forwards. The outside half does not want man and ball, nor does he want the ball with his forwards going backwards, but at the same time he must expect this to happen from time to time and learn to make good use of even a bad ball.

The ball should be put out in front of him so that he runs on to it and really gets his threequarters moving, A long quick pass from the scrum half is absolutely invaluable, but even so it will pay to vary his distance and angle of receiving the ball from his scrum half in order to unbalance the opposition flanker from a line-out.

With present laws, life for an outside half from a scrum is much more tolerable, because flank forwards simply cannot catch the outside half the way they used to do. However, Law 83 has given the outside half some extra work which he hadn't bargained for, because now he must tackle his opposite number.

A few years ago an outside half could leave his opposite number to the willing hands of his own flank forwards, but today an outside half who cannot tackle or is unwilling to tackle his opposite number is a luxury that most teams can ill afford. It is vital that the outside half gets up on to his opposite number as quickly as possible because if he doesn't there is a potential break possible between himself and his inside centre.

At the same time it is his job to make certain that the threequarters do come up on their opposite numbers as a unit and not like a dog's leg – the latter will only make defending extremely difficult and so present the opposition with opportunities for penetrating your back-line. It is worth illustrating the difference between ' running on to the ball ' and ' running with it ', because of the following reasons.

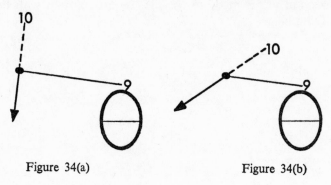

Figure 34(a)   Figure 34(b)

Running on to the Ball (Figure 34 (a))

Straight running, ball can be moved inside (forward support) or outside (your own threequarters).

Running with the Ball (Figure 34 (b))

The rest of your backs haven't a chance with this sort of running, unless you intend to switch the direction of play with your inside centre.

The outside half should help his scrum half by not asking him to pass too often in the opposite direction to the put-in. At the same time he should look for possibilities of using the short side of the field from rucks and mauls.

He, more than anyone, should realize that kicking loses possession, but that if he is kicking to touch from a defensive situation in his own twenty-five area, the ball must go into touch. His kicking in attack should in part nurse his forwards and, at the same time, expose the positional limitations of the opposition full back – put the ball into the open spaces and not down the full back's throat.

It follows that there will be very few occasions when he is not within passing distance of his scrum half and that he must expect rough treatment from flank forwards if ever he allows himself to be caught. He is not just there to shovel on the ball, but to mould the pattern of play so that the maximum use is made of the players around him with the ball that he gets.

12

Individual Skills

Throughout it has been stressed that any lack of skill in the individual players will have a detrimental effect on the performance of the team; therefore, the more skilful the individual players can make themselves, the better.

In the past, schoolmaster coaches have spent too much time on technique, and not enough time on applying the technique learned in game situations. It is one thing to demonstrate your techniques in practice without opposition, it is quite another thing to display them in a match. If you can do the latter, then it means that you are able to make and take decisions, and this is real individual skill. Skill, remember, implies economy of effort, economy of movement, co-ordination, automatic action.

The coach must know, of course, the technique involved, recognize it in a practice session, and in a match, and finally be able to diagnose faults and correct them. It is worth re-emphasizing that he would be well advised to make a point of telling the players why they are learning a skill and what they should be attempting to achieve in the many situations that occur during a rugby match.

This approach should encourage the players to think for themselves and ultimately ensure that they do make and take decisions with confidence. Remember, you do not want to produce a robot; it is the player who takes the field on a Saturday afternoon and not the coach.

As you will recall from Chapter Two, individual skills are either basic to all players or only applicable to certain players and therefore known as positional skills. They are now looked at under four main headings, namely, handling, running, contact and kicking.

Handling

As the word would suggest, how you transfer the ball from one player to another is immaterial, the essential thing to bear in mind is that the player receiving it must get it at the correct time, and in a position which gives him a reasonable chance of catching it. That position would normally be out in front – a key coaching point. When moving at speed, it is extremely difficult to take a ball by your shins or up near your head. It is easy to take a ball out in front of you at waist height; in other words a 'flat pass'. In this way the receiver of the ball immediately crosses the Gain Line (Key factor No 4).

Under the general skill of handling, there are three accepted types of pass, but one must not rule out any other type which proves effective.

1 *Drawing-a-man*

Figure 35

This figure shows the almost classic 2 v. 1 situation – the position that the attackers want to find themselves in and the defender does not. Player A must make certain that player C is committed. In other words A must persuade C to tackle him (A) and this is done by turning slightly to the inside of C so that the latter has to stop. Once this happens, it is a simple matter for A to swing the ball out in front of player B. This is the basic pass. Consider Plate Seven.

If C is experienced enough, he can (i) keep on the inside of A so that A is forced towards the touch-line and when he does pass the ball, C moves outwards and takes player B with ease. (ii) Move slightly to the outside of A's running line (dotted line) and by so doing make A think that he can dummy C and carry on running. Player C can then turn quickly into the path of A and tackle him head on or else with his right arm try to knock the ball out of A's hands. These two methods for defender C are very risky, but do work. However, it is simpler to remember the golden rule: *take the man with the ball – never take a dummy*.

One more coaching point; if you are trying to develop the rapid transfer of the ball along the back line, take the ball early. If each back does this and swings his arms, putting the ball out in front of the next man, then the ball will absolutely fizz along the line. With practice you can develop this method of transferring the ball to such a degree of perfection that you can catch and pass in the same stride.

Yet another method of transferring the ball along a back line is to catch the ball directly in front of your stomach – you are not taking it early this time – and then to move it on without any back swing of the arms by simply bringing the forearm and shoulder over the ball.

It is the force exerted by the opposite forearm and shoulder to the direction in which you pass the ball that gives the ball its impetus. This method has much to commend it on a wet day when the ball is heavy and slippery.

2 *Switch Pass*

As the word would indicate, the object of this type of pass is to switch the direction of the attack. If in figure 35 player A found that he was being forced towards the touch-line by the skill of player C's positioning, then it would be a simple matter for players A and B to effect a switch pass, like so.

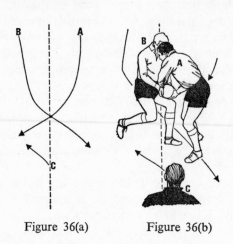

Figure 36(a)   Figure 36(b)

All you need to remember in a switch pass is to always *turn the ball in the direction of the man* who is going to take it. By doing this you automatically turn the ball away from and out of sight of the defender, player C. You will note that every player has been carrying the ball in two hands – an important coaching point. Only the player with exceptionally large hands can afford to discount this rule.

3 *Screen Pass*

The object of a screen is to hide something, a screen pass does exactly the same; it hides or screens the ball from a defender. As you saw when you read about the forwards as a unit, when they support each other in the loose they are essentially screening the ball for their own players by keeping it out of sight of the opposition.

There are two ways of doing this, one in the manner of the French, which involves turning before you get to an opponent, and so presenting him with your back, and the New Zealand method which involves direct shoulder contact, so that the opponent is knocked on to his heels. As this latter method is often the prelude to a ruck, this is the one I shall illustrate.

Figure 37(a)   Figure 37(b)

You will see how player A in figure 37(a) is driving in to make contact with player C and that the ball is now in a position ready for a short pop-up-pass because A has turned slightly after he has driven into the defender. Player B must time his arrival so that he accelerates at the moment the ball is transferred; the foward momentum will then not be lost.

It is not difficult to see how player A or B could so easily create a ruck in this situation if he felt he could not give the ball to a player in a better position. In figure 37(b) the ball is carried on the hip and slipped to the supporting player.

4 *The Catch – High Ball*
As this is discussed in some detail on pages 155 and

156 figures 38(a), 38(b) and 38(c) will complement the narrative on those pages.

Figure 38(a)
Eyes on the ball –
fingers spread

Figure 38(b)
Turn beginning

Figure 38(c)
Ball into body
for safety
Turn almost complete

5 *The Catch – Bouncing Ball*

This skill requires endless practice and demands that the eyes are firmly fixed on the ball. You will see from figure 39 that the catcher must not snatch at the ball, but judge its pace and bounce so that he can ride very slightly with the ball and so avoid the knock on.

Figure 39

6 *Picking the Ball Up*

Again, avoid snatching the ball or overplaying the rather

flashy one-handed pick-up. As always, two hands are safest, and the player should get his body over the ball.

One leg trails behind the ball so that if you fail to pick it up then this leg may be able to kick it on and thereby give you a second chance.

7 *Torpedo Throw*

One normally associates this type of throw with the line-out but if more players could throw accurately by this method there would be no reason why it should not be used in loose play for changing the point of attack.

As a method of throwing in to the line-out, it has many advantages. It can be thrown fast or slow, high or low, long or short, and if thrown correctly, then with geat accuracy.

The technique itself is simple. The ball, with the lace to the side, is rested on the palm of the hand with the thumb on the inside and fingers spread on the outside, reaching if possible to the lace. The elbow leads the throw and the spin is imparted as the fingers come down through the ball.

If the ball does not have a lace, and many obviously do not these days, then it is slightly harder to get the necessary purchase on the ball but certainly not impossible. All schoolboys should learn the technique with a small rugby ball; once learned it is relatively easy to apply this method with a full-size ball.

The important point for the coach is to realize why the ball is thrown in from above head height. The answer is simple. It is virtually the only position which gives the jumper a full view of the ball, and, therefore, he knows when to time his jump.

8 *Jumping, Catching and Wedging*

Anyone will see when reading about the locks in Chapter Nine that there is much more to jumping for the ball in a line-out than meets the eye. Ideally, we want to catch the ball with two hands so that we have maximum control over it, but this requires a high degree of skill.

It should also be pointed out that there are two positions in the line-out from which the ball is caught; (a) at the front, from positions two or three; (b) from the middle or back of the line-out, and that a slightly different technique is required.

(a) At the front

The jumper at two or three in fact takes the ball not above his head but in front of him. He turns as he takes it so that when he comes back to earth, he has his seat into the opposition.

Remember the two players on either side of the jumper cannot wedge in on him until the jumper has touched the ball. Even though the ball is going to be fed to the scrum half the wedge should be forceful and should aim to take the jumper forward. There are two accepted ways of wedging. The players on either side of the jumper bind their nearest arm round the waist of the jumper or between his thighs, like so.

Figure 40(a)   Figure 40(b)

Figure 40(a) difficult to bring the ball right down with two arms round the jumper's waist.

Figure 40(b) Easy to bring the ball down when binding between his thighs, because this method allows the jumper complete freedom to feed the ball to his scrum half.

(b) In the middle or at the back of the line-out

This time the ball is taken on the top of the jump, and it is either taken with two hands (difficult, but it can be done; the jumper can feed from this position directly to his scrum half) or from the inside arm (often the jumper can get higher with one hand than two) and then guided to the other hand and subsequently fed to the scrum half. The need for the jumper to turn and come down with his back to the opposition should again be emphasized. (See Plate 8.)

9 *Scrum Half – Spin Pass*

Bearing in mind that a man on the floor is a man out of the game, it would be advisable for coaches to concentrate on coaching the correct positional play, so that the scrum half does not have to resort to diving when he passes the ball. Once positional play is mastered, then the spin pass seems to give all the necessary qualities, namely, speed, length and accuracy. The spin is imparted from the top hand by bringing it through and across the ball.

Opposition
Loose
Forwards

Figure 41

This is illustrated in figure 41. You will note that the scrum half does not turn his back to the opposition loose forwards.

10 *Falling on the Ball*

There may be the odd occasion when you are forced to stop a forward rush by actually going forward to meet the ball, but this should be avoided because the risks involved are high. When the rush is under way, you would do far better to persuade the dribblers to over kick, by feigning a dive at their feet. Once the dribbler has kicked the ball past you it is then a simple matter to fall on it, and in the same movement be on your feet and backing into them.

Figure 42(a)   Figure 42(b)   Figure 42(c)

The essential part of the technique can be seen in figures 42(a), (b), (c). Ideally, you would time your fall and pick up so that as you forcefully back in to them they overshoot you. You will see that the faller has scooped the ball into his stomach with his right hand and at the same time is levering himself off the ground with his left. It is vital that you are on your feet immediately and this is a mental action which takes place even before you begin to fall. With practice, the one handed scoop can be as safe as two hands and infinitely quicker.

11 *Charging Down a Kick*

This is not normally deemed a skill, but when it is done properly, it most certainly is. It is included here because so many players jump into the air and turn their backs when trying to charge down a kick. These are both fundamental errors and present the kicker with a wonderful opportunity of producing a dummy kick. It takes courage, but you must go for the ball and not the kicker. The arms are outstretched and the elbows close together and slightly bent so that the ball cannot go between your forearms. Your face is protected by being behind your arms.

Running

Perhaps the most exciting of all the individual skills are the sidestep, swerve, and hand-off. These are essentially associated with running although the hand-off must in part be considered as a contact skill. No photograph really does justice to any of them, because it fails to capture the magic of what is essentially an act of deception.

12 *Sidestep*

In learning the technique of the sidestep, all you need to remember is that you transfer your weight from one foot to the other, but almost at a right angle.

This can be learnt at school in a modern education gymnastics lesson under the general theme of weight transference. Having learnt the technique the problem is to demonstrate it as a skill in a match. For some, there will be no problem, they will do it automatically; for the majority, however, it will require a conscious effort to get themselves in a position to demonstrate this skill. The defender must be made to misread your intentions, and this can be done by making him run in the opposite direction to which you intend to sidestep, or else by running at him, in order to catch him flat-footed so that you can take your choice as to which foot you use to sidestep off. Figure 43 shows how in the last few strides you can take the defender in the opposite direction to your intended sidestep.

Figure 43

(Your weight is gathered ready for the step to the left)

13 *The Swerve*

This is an extremely difficult skill to learn because you need to have excellent balance and a change of pace to make the swerve really effective. It looks simple, and it is fairly simple to describe, but immensely difficult to perform well. All you have to do is to lean to the inside of a would-be tackler with your shoulders, so that he is forced to check in his stride in case, in fact, you do go that way; you then change gear and accelerate away. It should be quite impossible for the defender to pick up his speed again.

14 *The Hand-off*

The skill of handing-off is normally associated with the wing, and consequently much of what needs to be said was in fact said in Chapter Eleven under the heading Wing Backs. The following drawing should suffice at this point.

Figure 44

(You use the would-be tackler's head to push yourself further away from him)

Contact

You cannot avoid contact in rugby, so it is as well to be mentally prepared for it, physically strong, and technically competent to carry out what is required of you.

15 *Shoulder Charge*

In this instance, I am not thinking of the shoulder contact that soccer players are allowed, but the direct forward thrust which some players use to remove an opponent from their path. This is a perfectly legitimate and mighty effective way of making progress to the opponent's goal line. At the same time, it is not the sole prerogative of the sixteen stone forward, and to be done properly it requires to be perfectly timed.

There is little point in dipping your shoulder and driving into an opponent if he is expecting it. If he is a player of any ability, he will bring you to earth quite comfortably by executing a front tackle, in which he merely sits and falls backward, allowing your own weight to bring you to the ground.

Again, you would be advised to run slightly to his outside, and at the last moment drive hard diagonally into him. This is not the sort of skill you practise in cold blood, but you will find that some players discover its effectiveness for themselves. It has rather cogently been referred to as a *Maori side-step* in New Zealand by way of a tribute to the strength of many Maori rugby players.

Tackling

All you have to remember in tackling is that no one can run with their legs together, and even if you do not execute the perfect tackle – hang on!

16 *Side Tackle*

You should be trying to drive your shoulder into a point between his knee and thigh, with your head tucked safely behind his seat. However, as the person you are tackling will almost certainly be running, make certain you aim for this area, but at least two feet the other side of him. This will ensure that you are not left grasping for his ankles as he breaks free of your attempted tackle. If you find he has enormous thighs, allow your arms to slide down to his knees or shins, which should be thinner!

17 *Front Tackle*

Here you aim to take the tackled player over a shoulder, then all you have to remember is hang on – sit – fall backwards (his weight and speed will bring him down) and turn to end up on top (see figures 45(a), (b) and (c)).

Figure 45(a)

Figure 45(b)

Figure 45(c)

18 *Smother Tackle*

This is the sort of tackle that takes place at close quarters, or if the poor unfortunate full back is all that remains between an opponent and the goal line. In the latter situation in particular, a low tackle would almost certainly still allow the man carrying the ball to fall forward and score and so you must either bring your shoulder up sharply into his stomach to stop him, or try to pin his arms to the side so that the ball is trapped between the two of you. If you can, you would also attempt to turn him as you both fall backwards towards the goal line, so that you end up on top.

19 *Rear Tackle*

As with the side tackle, your aim must be beyond the tackled player, in order to make contact with him, remember he will be moving away from you. Your arms encircle him round about hip height, but as he comes to earth, your arms will automatically slide down to knee height. It is particularly important that you grip his legs firmly so that his heels can do you no damage.

20 *Ankle-tap*

If you are chasing a player, and it is obvious that you will never get near enough to him to execute a rear tackle, then there is just the chance that you can still bring him down if you can tap his trailing ankle towards the other.

It must be the trailing ankle because this is the one without any weight on it. Once you knock it towards the other he will come to earth in a most undignified manner.

21 *The Tackled Player*

So often when learning to tackle, the ball is completely forgotten, yet it is of the utmost importance. A man who is being tackled must immediately think of putting the ball where it can be seen by the supporting players of his own side. This will usually be behind him. In any event, the ball must not shoot forward or be trapped beneath him. If he can turn as he is falling, and land on his back, then he is perfectly entitled to pass the ball from this position, thus:

Figure 46, this is not defined as having been tackled

At the worst, he should end up between the ball and the opposition. Naturally, if he can roll clear, then he must do so (Law 18). (See Plate 9.)

22 Shoving in a Scrum

Shoving in the scrum is too often misguidedly forgotten or not considered to be a skill. The two important points for player and coach are (a) Chin Up, this helps to flatten your back, and (b) Feet Apart with the inside leg back at roughly an angle of 45° from the vertical and the outside leg forward, that is if you are a prop. The lock often has both of his legs back at this angle.

Generally weight is applied from the inside of your feet like so

Figure 47(a) and not Figure 47(b)

The latter method imposes too much strain on your achilles tendon, calf and hamstring muscles, and is not so efficient because you do not have so much purchase on the ground. You should be comfortable, and to be comfortable, it helps if you are strong.

K

Kicking

There has always been a place in the game for accurate kicking, and I am sure there always will be, but the very shape of the ball ensures that unless your technique is sound, then your kicking will not be accurate. The one thing you must not do when kicking out of your hand is to throw the ball upwards. Use two hands and think of either dropping or placing the ball on to your foot, this will give you some measure of control over the ball; and like the golfer, keep your head down.

23 *Screw Kick*

There is little point in talking about a punt when the screw kick is easy to learn, far more accurate, and will travel further:

Figure 48(a)   Figure 48(b)   Figure 48(c)

(i) Holding the ball. Figure 48(a).
(ii) Complete right footed kick. Figure 48(b).
(iii) A right footed screw kick in this situation will give distance and accuracy that a punt could not equal. Figue 48(c).

(Note the straight leg just after the ball has been struck.)

24 'Up and Under' and Cross Kick

These two types of kick are grouped together because they both require height and because the height is acquired by keeping the knee bent after having kicked the ball (the opposite to the screw kick). They are, however, usually executed by different players; the former by the scrum half or outside half and the latter by a wing. They must be practised and preferably in game situations.

To generalize about kicking, a straight leg will give distance, a bent leg (knee) will give height.

25 Drop Kick

This sort of kick is used to re-start a game from the half-way or as a result of a drop-out twenty-five. In these two situations, you are entitled to practise in a rather static situation, but if you want to score goals with this sort of kick then you need to practise with at least one opponent. In a game, time is a luxury which you rarely get. The ball is dropped from out in front of you, and kicked with the top surface of your instep, just after the point of the ball has struck the ground. The ball is in fact on its way back up.

It is vital that you drop the ball in such a way that your instep fits under it. You rarely hit the ball square on, but swing slightly from the side into it. Not only is this a more natural position, but it helps you to get greater distance.

26 Grubber Kick

The backs are the players who generally use the grubber kick when the opposition are coming up on them quickly. It is rather like the drop kick except that (a) the ball is kicked from much nearer the body, (b) the instep is nearer the vertical and (c) the ball never leaves the ground.

The aim is to place the ball between the oncoming players so that one of your team mates can run on to it.

27 *Place Kick*

Any method that is successful is worthy of consideration, although the well tried and more orthodox method is illustrated here. A controlled, slightly accelerated run up which is absolutely straight seems to give the best results.

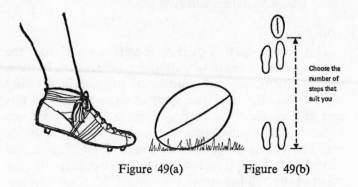

Choose the number of steps that suit you

Figure 49(a)   Figure 49(b)

Figure 49(a) You must be able to see the point of the ball.

Figure 49(b) Choose the number of strides that suits you.

28 *Dribbling*

Dribbling is not often used these days, but it is certainly an extremely valuable skill to possess on a wet day. Control is kept with the inside of the feet, and it is important that the ball should be kept fairly close to the dribbler and that his support should be positioned to continue the movement if the player leading the dribble overshoots the ball. You must be balanced.

29 *Hooking*

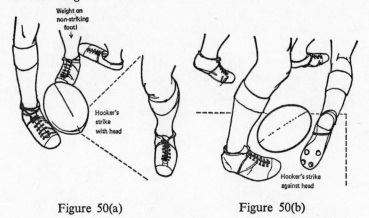

Figure 50(a)   Figure 50(b)

(1) Weight on non-striking foot, (2) The strike or deflection, figure 50(a); (3) Against the head, figure 50(b).

You will see from figure 50(a) that the ball is deflected by the hooker down the channel made by his pack. When he strikes against the head, figure 50(b), he generally needs the assistance of his tighthead prop to follow the ball in with his outside foot.

Finally, the important point for coach and player is to remember that once you have mastered a part or all of the technique then you should think of practices which are as near to the real game situation as possible. Only then can you hope to add another individual skill to your repertoire.

Special
Subjects

13

Mental and Physical Fitness

A rather familiar advertisement begins: 'When you wake up in the morning do you feel lethargic or depressed?' What follows here is not intended as a commercial, but simply to illustrate that every person is subject to many different feelings. Yet, when you arrive at the ground on a match afternoon, some of these feelings may have to be overcome if they are not to conflict with the best interests of the team.

In a sense you live your life in a series of compartments and each of these compartments will demand your attention and efforts in varying ways. The periods of time that you set aside for rugby training, practice and playing will make specific demands on you mentally and physically and therefore will have to be arranged with the general routine of your life so that they cause the minimum of inconvenience and give the maximum of pleasure.

For example, you come home worn out after a hard day – it's the club practice night. Naturally enough your initial reaction is that you do not feel like making the effort. But if you think that way, so may the rest of your team. Remember, to have a successful team there must be a feeling of collective responsibility.

You decide to go to the club practice session – Here is the crunch! You must now mentally discipline yourself for one to one and a half hours of concentrated effort. Of course it will be hard, but it should also be rewarding (captains and coaches take note) and if you have got this far, do not waste your time, or more important, the time of the other fourteen players by fooling on. This is not the time or the place. It will all be worthwhile come Saturday.

Even at this point you will see the need for self discipline, but this is only a part of what goes towards making a player mentally fit. In the rugby context, mental fitness must therefore incorporate self discipline plus the following. Mental hardness (never admitting defeat and not being intimidated), quickness of thought, the ability to concentrate and finally, developing the ability to react automatically.

Some days you will not feel like playing, others you will be raring to go, but somehow or other you have to conquer the former feelings for the sake of the team. This is always a problem for captain and coach and this is where psychology, kidology, or motivational techniques are used in practice sessions, pre-match warm-ups and dressing room talks.

It no doubt seems all very childish to the uninitiated and even to the players at times, but if everyone is going to give of their best for the team, then everyone has to be sufficiently alive mentally to want to play as well as they possibly can and produce a winning effort.

I always remember asking a schoolboy the following question: ' What were the opposition like today?' and he replied, ' They had some good players, but they did not want to win as much as we did.' Rightly or wrongly I was delighted with his answer because I felt it showed that at least one of the team was beginning to think and feel the opposition.

What a psychological advantage this lad's team had, or indeed any team has, when it senses that it wants to win more than its opponents. This feeling is very apparent in New Zealand and South African players.

The part that intimidation plays in rugby is probably extremely small but a captain or a coach should be aware of it. Very rarely are threats turned into actions, but occasionally words from the lips of a grizzly unshaven forward have had petrifying effects on players whose size of body belies their size of heart. Quite obviously if you are thinking of what an opponent might do to you then you cannot be concentrating on the job in hand; that is to get the ball.

The player who thinks quickly is worth his weight in gold – the Gareth Edwards short penalty to Denzil Williams for a Welsh try against Ireland in 1969 is a wonderful example of what I mean (the opposition had turned their backs in anticipation of a kick at goal), but, of course, there are many more and they occur in all grades of rugby. It doesn't have to be the prerogative of the international player to think quickly.

I suppose self discipline and the ability to concentrate go hand in hand and a lack of concentration on the field, especially, is so obvious to the discerning spectator. The forward who is in front of the kicker at the start of a match, or at a drop out. The winger who misreads the line-out signal and throws to the wrong man. The player who makes a gorgeous break and streaks up the field only to ruin his effort by throwing the ball away, and usually to an opponent who immediately starts a counter attack in the opposite direction.

There are many more examples all equally as frustrating to the team as to the spectators. British players seem to have been sufferers of more than their fair share of such misfortunes. When will they ever learn?

Lastly we come to reactions which are automatic. By carefully thinking about the task at hand and the role that each individual player has, everyone is capable of turning the normal conscious actions on the field of play into subconscious actions. For example, most players go through the stage of learning to catch a high ball without dropping it – eyes on the ball, and elbows in. You then realize, or are taught, to half turn as you take a high ball so that even if you do not catch it cleanly at least you will not knock it on.

These are all very definite and conscious efforts at the start, but gradually you will do them automatically and start moving to the stage when you can not only do this, but make a mental note of how many players from the opposition are following up the kick and where they are placed in relation to you. In other words, you will already have planned your next move after having caught and half turned with the ball. This sort of thought process can be applied to any skill or situation where skills are needed.

From all of this you will have gathered that mental fitness is a very wide subject, but of tremendous importance and it is obvious that mental fitness in the rugby context ensures that the player is totally aware of what is happening around him and able to respond accordingly.

Whoever said ' You are as fit as it takes you time to recover ' very neatly summed up many of the problems associated with acquiring a high level of physical fitness. Of course, it is not the whole answer, but for the layman who is trying to raise his degree of physical fitness, it can be a reasonable efficient method of measuring any improvement in his performance, provided he is honest with himself.

This is very simply illustrated. You run a measured 100 yards in eleven seconds. You find it takes you five minutes before you can repeat this distance in the same time. As soon as you can do the 100 yards in eleven seconds with less than five minutes rest you must be getting fitter.

Unfortunately playing a game of rugby is not as simple as running a straight 100 yards and here it would be as well to briefly state the conditions which would guide our training and practice programme. Obviously we need speed, strength, power (applied strength) and stamina, but they are not used in any gradual and economic way because the very nature of the game produces a wide variety of situations where our physical resources are needed in fits and starts.

One minute a player may be pushing in a scrum, wrestling for the ball in a maul, sprinting, tackling or being tackled, under a heap of players, swerving to beat an opponent or kicking a ball. Just about every part of his anatomy is being used and it goes without saying that he has to be physically resilient as well as fit if he is to last the full eighty minutes.

In athletics, swimming or soccer, the work load and rate

of work that performers have been putting in over the last few years has increased sharply and the outcome has often resulted in world records being shattered or, in the case of soccer, a very much faster game. The human frame is an incredible piece of machinery and if sufficiently motivated can perform prodigious feats. However, the result is that many non-professional athletes are having to spend two or three hours of each day, sometimes longer, to produce the desired effect; let us say a world record.

If rugby players were going to spend the same amount of time in training and practice to raise their standards to a comparable level, the situation would get right out of hand because obviously few can work an eight or nine hour day for five days of the week and keep up this amount of training and practice over the course of an eight-month rugby season. Nor, I suspect, would they have such a long career as rugby players.

The problem for coach and captain therefore is to discover just how little each individual player has to do in order to reach his own optimum of physical fitness. I suppose a player will be influenced in finding this optimum physical fitness level by first of all asking himself what he wants from rugby union football.

If he is extremely ambitious then he will have to be prepared to work more readily at improving his physical fitness, if he is not ambitious then presumably his physical fitness level will be correspondingly lower. One occasionally hears a player described as being over-trained but rarely is this the result of too much physical exercise. More often than not he is suffering from mental fatigue brought on as a result of a lack of variety in his training and practice programme. Coaches take note.

Although I am now going to concern myself with the player who wants to get fit and keep fit in his own time, the following training methods are universal and should be understood by the school and club coach alike and more important tailored to meet the requirements of an individual or a team. Remember, training should be progressive, that is you must aim to gradually increase the amount and intensity of your training and not attempt too much in the early stages.

The prerequisite of any physical activity is to have strength and the easiest and most efficient way of acquiring strength is by weight training. Ideally your club or school would have a set of weights and somebody who could explain and supervise the lifting of them. (The coach.) Lifting weights can be dangerous if in the hands of people who attempt to outlift one another – this by the way is not weight training, but weight lifting.

Briefly, the principle you need to remember is the overload principle – that is, additional strength can only be achieved if the load is constantly increased. Therefore (i) heavy weights and few repetitions leads to a gain in strength, (ii) light weights and more repetitions leads to a gain in muscular endurance. If you do not have access to a weight training set, then the following can be used; concrete set in old film cans, buckets filled with stones or bricks, heavy books for arm exercises or added resistance when doing trunk curls and sit ups. The possibilities of make-shift equipment are unlimited provided you use your initiative.

Ideally you would do your weight training in the summer where you would have the time and opportunity to build up strength for the winter. All players regardless of their position would benefit from weight training, but they would be well advised never to undertake it without receiving competent instruction. Having acquired strength through weight training you now have to apply your strength to the maximum effect on the rugby field. This is simply demonstrated if we look at a maul and a ruck.

A maul is usually a fairly static situation which demands strength to tear the ball from the hands of an opponent or to smuggle the ball between members of your own team. On the other hand to win a ball at a ruck requires applied strength that is power.

Power is the ability to move a resistance at speed and quite obviously if your rucking is going to be effective then you will have to move the resistance, that is the opposition's forwards, in order to win the ball.

Speed and stamina can be acquired in a number of ways; *fartlek* running can be especially pleasant. *Fartlek* is a Swedish word meaning speed play and *fartlek* running is best done in a park or wood or over sand-dunes. In this type of running the athlete runs literally as he feels like it, alternating between very slow or very fast, but obviously he must make certain that he does not overdo the slow, otherwise there will be little real benefit.

He is really playing with speed and if he can find some uphill stretches these should help his leg strength whilst downhill runs should give him an opportunity of developing his leg speed. For the player training by himself there is little of the drudgery associated with running round a rugby pitch because there should be plenty of changes of scenery.

On the other hand interval running is a little more restricted, although it does aim to progressively build up a person's speed, stamina and will power. The last point being of particular importance. The intervals being run would probably vary from widths to lengths to circuits of a rugby field. The rest period would be just sufficient to allow the player to run the fast intervals again at the correct speed.

The player would select the number of intervals he intends to run before he commences his training – the need for will power becomes apparent as he carries out the last two or three intervals.

How do you check your progress? (a) You should take less time to recover between intervals; (b) You should gradually increase the speed of your intervals of running. A simple check that you can use for timing your rest period is to start running again when your pulse has come back down to 120.

On the other hand if you want to work hard (i) take your normal pulse, say 60; (ii) your pulse rate after severe exercise, say 200; (iii) the range equals 200 − 60 that is 140; (iv) assuming 140 represents 100% range of your capacity and you wish to work to 50% of this capacity, that's 70; (v) add this 70 to your normal pulse rate, that is 70 + 60 equals 130; (vi) when your pulse rate comes back down to 130, you start your fast interval again.

This formula is often used by swimming and athletic coaches. Another useful way of building up your speed and endurance is by doing acceleration runs. For example, using the length of a street or lap of rugby pitch, gradually build up your speed so that the last fifty yards is at full speed. You should try and develop a relaxed yet firm running style.

If you are concerned about your lack of stamina, then running in heavy boots or in sand are both simple and useful ways of rectifying this deficiency. Also you could easily embark on a course of circuit training without the need for any fancy gym equipment.

It is so simple to arrange and organize a circuit in your own home by using, for example, a chair for step-ups or better still the hall stairs, a door for pull-ups, two buckets filled with stones or sand for arm exercises, etc. In circuit training you usually perform eight to ten repetitions of each exercise and go round your chosen circuit three times. For full particulars you should read *Circuit Training* by Morgan and Adamson, published by G. Bell & Sons Ltd.

The coach with a physical education background will be familiar with tests and measurements and many of the tests used in the physical education syllabus can prove both enjoyable and motivating to the player, particularly if his scores are recorded.

For the individual player one of the simplest tests to use is a modified version of the US Navy test which only takes thirteen minutes from beginning to end.

The programme is:

 1 minute maximum BURPEES
 1 minute Rest
 1 minute maximum PRESS UPS
 1 minute Rest
 1 minute BURPEE JUMPS
 2 minutes Rest
 2 minutes SIT-UPS
 3 minutes Rest
 1 minute SQUAT JUMPS.

Average scores to guide you:

SCHOOLBOYS (16-17 yrs)

	Burpees	P. Ups	B. Jumps	Sit-Ups	Squat Jumps
Average	28	6	24	44	40
Good	36	13	34	60	55

The schoolboy figure here is for pull ups *not* press ups.

CLUB PLAYERS

Burpees	P. Ups	B. Jumps	Sit-Ups	Squat jumps
30	34	25	65	40

You will note that quite often the fit schoolboys score better than the average club player.

To end this section let me quote Ivan Vodanovich, the present All Blacks' coach, and the sort of pre-season training schedule he was asking his Wellington players to carry out.

1 Place tremendous emphasis on training for rugby, speak from a position of strength and fitness.
2 Rugby players' capacities have never been measured, nor are we to judge what they can do by any precedents, so little has been tried.
3 Rugby players the country over should now engage in a search for the kind of fitness that will give a pull over the other fellow.

L

4 Work out a six-week schedule now and optimistically carry it out each week.

A six-week schedule
Monday morning: (before breakfast) 30 minutes jogging.
Tuesday: 30 minutes strength building work.
Wednesday night: 30 minutes PT, jogging, sprinting.
Thursday: 30 minutes strength building work.
Friday: Rest.
Saturday: Sprinting 20 minutes; PT 20 minutes; jogging 30 minutes. Total 70 minutes.
Sunday: Rest.

All of this is in aid of the expected challenge of a new season.

We have seen on page 158 that the application of the overload principle will give you increased strength and Ivan Vodanovich has further suggestions for those who do not have access to proper weight training equipment and yet wish to increase their strength. He also has some interesting thoughts on what is needed in the modern game.

' Squats, which can be performed by repetitions of ten with 100lb of stones in a sugar bag on your back, should be done for ten of the thirty minutes (reference strength building). The remaining twenty minutes should be used for what I think is the best exercise outside running for a rugby player, dead lifting. The twenty minutes of dead lifting should be five repetitions of ten with a few minutes spell in between.

' The equipment for dead lifting is two four-gallon tins filled with sand or shingle joined together by a four to five foot piece of galvanized one inch pipe. The pipe can be pushed through one inch holes near the top of the tins, this brings the pipe about eighteen inches off the ground.

' Players will be amazed themselves just what heavy weights they can lift off the ground, once they have hardened themselves up after a couple of weeks. Even though they will be lifting this weight only from a knees bend to a knees straight action, the arms, legs, back, neck and chest all get worked over, if you make it heavy enough.

' I believe in the arms getting thrashed, because they are used so much in modern rugby.

' That extra lasting strength to rip the ball from an opponent, that durable power to push yourself, not only to your limit, but to something I believe a dedicated rugby player can develop, pushing yourself beyond your limit. A rugby player can double his arm strength in the off season with dead lifts alone.

' For the ones that say, " Where can we keep these contraptions?" – In the basement of your home, in the light well – of most buildings at work – in their building basements, or outside on the section. The shingle, galvanized pipe and tins do not rust or rot (tins are cheap anyway). To get more weight the sand and shingle only has to be wetted down.

' I'm a firm believer in less repetitions and more weight – ten reps of three hundred pounds is better than twenty of one hundred and fifty pounds.'

I think you will agree that to carry out this schedule and make you own strength building equipment, is not asking the impossible of any rugby player.

14

Introducing the Game

The purpose of this chapter is not to give a detailed stage by stage account of how the game must be introduced, but rather to stress just how vitally important the introduction is, and to outline those factors which appear to play an important part if the game is to be successfully introduced.

The starting point must be *enjoyment*. If a boy does not enjoy his introduction to rugby then there is every chance that he will be lost to the game for good. From this it is fairly obvious that if you begin by picking two teams of fifteen boys each and attempt to play a full game, there is little likelihood that any enjoyment will be experienced, because in this sort of introduction a boy would be lucky to see the ball, let alone handle it.

It would appear that schoolmasters often derive most success, and boys the greatest enjoyment, when rugby is introduced through small team games. Handling and running are such natural activities that all a boy needs to know is that tries are scored by placing the ball down over a goal line.

He wants to feel involved, he wants to score tries and by playing small team games, two v two, three v three, in a small area, then he will really feel that he is doing something worthwhile. All those who are introduced to the game by touching the ball once every fifteen minutes have every right to feel disappointed – this need never happen.

Provided you have a number of rugby balls, one master can cope with a large group of boys in a relatively small area, for example, the twenty-five. The twenty-five is subdivided into smaller areas simply by using flag-posts or jerseys as markers.

The games session is best organized in the form of a competition, for example, the winner of area one, moves to area two; the winner of area two moves to area three, etc. The overall winner at the end of the lesson is the team that has moved the farthest. A competition gives the activity some purpose and this is important to bear in mind.

Obviously there are many activities that could take place in each of the areas and there are also many ways of making the activity competitive, but do remember everybody should be involved in running and handling and scoring tries.

Even during this introductory stage many of the key coaching points can be introduced like, ' carry the ball in two hands ', ' ball out in front ', ' go forward ', etc. By using the correct terminology, the correct attitudes to the game can be cultivated. Generally the first stumbling block is tackling. Tackling involves contact and partner or group activities where there is some form of contact can often be an invaluable preliminary to learning the actual techniques of tackling.

Most physical education masters are familiar with activities like, King of the Ring, Armadas, Break-out, Chinese Boxing, and Four Cornered Tug-of-War. All of these have an element of contact in them, but it should also be pointed out that some boys will not be suited to any contact activity, no matter how mild its form or how well it is introduced. Consequently they will not be suited to a full game of rugby.

Certainly try to avoid situations where an eleven-year-old, weighing five and a half stones, has to stop a boy of the same age but weighing two stones heavier. In schools where games are organized so that a whole year is out at once, it is quite possible to grade the boys according to their stature; this is particularly important with young boys.

Another popular way of introducing the game, especially when the boys have only previously known the game of soccer, is to use this game as a starting point. At a given moment boys can be encouraged to pick the ball up and run with it. If they can place it on the ground over the goal line before being stopped, then they score three points – if they score a normal soccer goal, then it is one point.

Many will soon see that by picking up the ball and running, there is a greater chance of their team winning the game. From there you can introduce the heel between the legs after a stoppage, then move to a three man scrum and so the game begins to take shape.

Avoid telling boys new to the game, that there are twenty-seven laws to be mastered; this is a certain guarantee that their enthusiasm will wane. The Laws should arise and be introduced quite naturally as a result of one side gaining an unfair advantage. The purpose of a law should be explained in this context.

Whatever method is used to introduce the game, one thing is certain, the master will have to prepare his material thoroughly and through sound organization put it into practice. Poor facilities, perhaps only having one pitch, need be no obstacle, even with a large number of boys and little help; provided there are plenty of rugby balls available and the work has been prepared.

As the introduction to the game progresses, then interest is further stimulated by watching the school first team and if possible, club, county and international rugby. Rugby films and visits from rugby personalities (there is often someone living locally) should also be encouraged. Boys want to see how a school activity is related to outside events.

Finally, for those schoolmaster coaches who want to read much more deeply on this aspect of the game, they would be well advised to purchase a book on this very subject published by the Rugby Football Union at Twickenham.

15

The Pyramid

Throughout this book, stress has been given to everyone understanding the philosophy and concepts of the game, being able to recognize and implement the key factors and finally the importance of working from a common framework. However, it would appear that many people find it very difficult to grasp the importance of these points because they feel that there must be such an enormous gulf between playing for a school team and playing for a national or British Isles team.

Of course there are differences, but the important thing is that there are many more similarities, or there ought to be. The main differences are:

(i) Reaction time – in other words even the slightest lack of mental or physical speed has an adverse effect.

(ii) Mistakes cost points – drop a pass, miss a tackle and your team will suffer.

(iii) The psychological factors can be more complex, e.g. pre-match build-up in newspapers or television, playing in front of a 70,000 crowd. Difficulties of communication because of crowd noise, etc (these can all affect the players).

In school or club rugby you might be lucky and have a second chance; in international rugby this is most unlikely to happen.

The similarities on the other hand are many, the philosophy, concepts, key factors, individual, unit and team skills are identical and this should give heart to any aspiring player who previously had seen a county or international cap as being well out of his reach.

The structure of British rugby looks simple on paper, as illustrated in figure 51.

Figure 51

Underlying the pyramid, that is the whole game, should be the concepts and framework, this is vital. When it is realized that approximately 97% of all rugby players learn the game at school, the importance of this level is obvious. Whatever you learn at school tends to stick with you and later on it is often extremely difficult for a club coach to eradicate bad habits acquired during this school period.

This is why schoolmasters have always had and will continue to have a major part to play in shaping British rugby. They must teach the individual, unit and team skills thoroughly and begin to develop a pattern of play that will be effective and can be used later on against foreign opposition because if they do not then there is little likelihood that any of these things will be achieved by a few coaches working in isolation at international level. The transformation must come from the schools and work upwards.

However, it is accepted that an attractive and effective shop-window (a national side) has a most stimulating effect and may well in fact influence the pattern that is developed at school level. Operating within each school and club is a further pyramid, the apex of which is the school or club 1st XV.

In school the channels along which the players move are well defined. Various age groups and the vigilance of school-masters virtually ensure that each player finds his correct level. In club rugby the channels are less clearly defined even though a club may have a grading of teams from 1st XV to tenth XV. Quite often promotion to the 1st XV is a diffi-cult and chancy business for a wide variety of reasons.

There is the gulf between school and club rugby to be bridged, this may take time. Sometimes clubs with a large number of teams have the greatest difficulty in keeping the lines of communication connected.

A promising schoolboy player who gets his first run out with a club 8th or 9th XV may never be seen or heard of again, unless a team coach, captain or manager takes the trouble to report honestly and fairly on the prospects of this player. One hears stories, and I hope they are only stories, of over-zealous captains who are more concerned with the success of their own 8th or 9th XV than the future progress of a promising player. The latter's promise is conveniently forgotten when the club sides are picked at the beginning of the week.

Whilst it is important and desirable that captains of lower sides should want to have good playing results, the overall success of a club or school tends to be measured by the re-sults of the respective 1st XVs and if the first fifteens are not doing well because they do not contain the best players then something is radically wrong. The cream must not only come to the top of its own volition, it must also be encour-aged in every possible way.

Obviously not every player in club rugby wants to reach

the apex of the pyramid, their reasons for playing the game will be many and varied and this is how it should be, but the onus is on each club to see that it knows which of its players are ambitious and that those players find themselves playing in the appropriate team, with people of similar ambition and ability.

Looking around one can see examples of clubs that have been thinking and acting along these lines over the last few years, because they are now running successful colts teams (to cater for the school leavers at fifteen) and also because they have introduced either an under 21 or under 23 side; some clubs have even introduced all three grades.

If the structure of the pyramid within a school or club is correct then players with the necessary ability and drive will progress accordingly. To complement this upward movement of players, there should be a coaching programme and coaches who are capable of implementing it. A coach in the wrong position, and not sure of his role, is just as lethal as a player who finds himself in a similar predicament. It is difficult to make comment at club level, because I suspect that few clubs have a coaching programme, let alone a coach for every team.

At school level the situation is different because a large number of masters in charge of rugby do have a scheme of work and fellow masters (coaches) to help them. However, few masters in charge of rugby would think of giving a copy of the syllabus to each school coach or get them together to explain and show them not only what to teach and coach, but how to do it.

Yet if the coaching programme is to have the maximum impact then these sort of things must happen or else the supposed pyramid takes on an odd shape.

Assuming every player and coach is in the right position at school and club level, then the next step up the pyramid to county and regional level will be straightforward. If things do go wrong quite often key factor No 6, *Selection,* is a major contributor. County pride and area representation must be swallowed when picking the regional team.

Only the best county players should be picked and if they all happen to come from one county then the other counties should not take umbrage, but be determined to raise their own standards in the future. This also applies at national and British Isles level.

If the best players are going to reach the top at all levels then there is no room for sentiment. Similarly if coaching and coaches are to play their rightful part in the pyramid, channels will have to be found for the ablest to find their way up to the apex.

16

Role of
a Team Manager

It is always a sad day when a sportsman retires, and regrettably too many leave their particular sport, never to be seen or heard of again. Others, of course, give sterling service to their club as administrators, or help more generally by becoming referees.

The awareness that the playing standards at club level could be increased through coaching has in recent years brought more ex-rugby players in close contact with the game, as coaches. Some clubs have also realized the importance of each team in their club having a manager, so that the captain and coach can devote more time to coaching and not have to be concerned with the playing kit, the half-time oranges, why certain players missed a practice session, and the like.

This is not a case of creating a job for someone, the work is already there, and a clear cut division of labour has many advantages for all concerned, especially the players. The position of team manager can bring or keep an ex-player in close contact with the players and the game. This feeling of commitment and of having an important part to play makes viewing on a match day just that bit more exciting and worthwhile.

Before outlining the duties that a team manager might have, it is worth stating the following:

(i) Often old administrators are reluctant to chase after youth, because ' it wasn't like that in my day '. They sometimes forget that no game lives in the past and the future must lie in the hands of the young. The present generation having been weaned on the Welfare State and the affluent society find that there are many sports and activities that are open to them. They expect things to be well organized and no sport can sit back and expect youth to come flocking to it – a certain amount of selling has to be done. A manager can help to streamline the running of a team and indirectly make the game and that particular club more attractive to prospective players.

(ii) Most clubs have a fixture secretary, baggage man, and first-aid attendant, and so many of the items listed may already be covered.

(iii) The list is provided by Ivan Vodanovich and again is an insight into the thoroughness of New Zealand rugby.

TEAM MANAGER'S DUTIES

1 Collect players' valuables before each game.
2 Supply oranges.
3 Make sure all players are neatly attired with clean boots, jersey, socks and shorts.
4 Look after injured players. Report injuries to club captain without delay. No specialist treatment without club's approval. Obtain referee's chit for injury.
5 Keep a supply of team sheets.
6 Collect players' subscriptions and pay to treasurer.
7 Give results of game to assistant secretary or secretary by Saturday night.
8 Ensure that ball is available and at the right pressure for each game, and be responsible for the safety of the ball after each game. Make sure that playing and practice balls are the right pressure. Footballs to be sole responsibility of the manager.
9 Ring all players who miss practice, and report to coach.
10 Organize all transport to football games.
11 Assist coach to present his full previous year's team to

club captain one week before commencement of first
training run.

12 Collect all club's gear, such as jersey, socks and shorts
after game.

13 Be responsible for laundry of team's gear.

14 First aid kits to be sole responsibility of manager.

15 Check eligibility to play for your team, e.g. if necessary
has a transfer from another club been approved, is the
player within the prescribed age group for his grade?

16 Attend all practices with coach.

17 Ensure that team's emergency gear such as shorts, jersey,
socks, laces, garters, hammer and pliers are readily available on Saturdays.

18 The manager is responsible for the full team's current
addresses and phone numbers. They must be kept up-to-
date.

19 Make sure players are informed of all club functions,
social and otherwise team or club.

20 Availability of all managers/coaches/players three
games before end of season for next season.

21 Maintain contact at least twice during off season with
previous season's players with view to keeping fit.

22 Attend coaching and other meetings where coach unable
to attend.

23 Organize visitors to hospitalized injured players.

Conclusion

17
Looking Ahead

How many times have we heard pundits of the game tell us that the recent touring side was the best that ever visited these shores? That this school or that club will never produce sides of such high quality again?

This has happened on many occasions and whilst we ought to learn from touring sides and from playing against individual players, schools and clubs who are better than ourselves, we must also be aware of the great danger of living in the past and in becoming purely copiers and not originators.

To win any game you have basically to outwit the opposition and for far too long now we have half-heartedly met the increasingly fierce challenge of New Zealand, South Africa, France and latterly Argentina, Romania, Fiji and Japan, without applying our wits to countering their pattern of play. Only by such application can one evolve an original and effective counter, in other words, one cannot supply the answer without analysing the problem.

To say that we are too preoccupied with New Zealand, South Africa and France in particular is to evade the issue and it may well be that we shall have to take from each of these countries the better aspects of their game and add to them our flair for the unorthodox, which we have on occasions so tantalizingly demonstrated as being our real strength. Regrettably, we have been afraid to experiment and have been drawn into the trap of playing safe with the inevitable result.

In the preceding text, whilst it is hoped that a framework for success has been outlined to player, captain and coach,

M

it is also hoped that sufficient room has been left for every-one to develop their own ideas within this framework. To illustrate a few of the areas in which there is scope for original thought, the following are offered for consideration.

At the beginning of a game, one side is presented with the ball for the kick-off and invariably kicks straight to their opponents; this usually ends in a scrum. Some sides kick the ball dead and then have a chance of regaining possession when the opposition take the twenty-five drop out. This in-dicates a certain amount of thought, but there must be many more moves possible from the kick-off which keep the ball away from the opposition forwards and still in play.

Twenty-five drop-outs are rarely taken quickly enough and the open spaces are insufficiently used. Not enough use is made of the whole of the twenty-five yard line; too often the kick is taken from the middle and only after the opposi-tion have been allowed to prepare themselves to receive the ball. It is rather like the kick-off ritual.

The only stipulation on the scrum is that there shall be no more than three players in the front row. Whilst it is difficult to get the ball with less than eight players it ought to be easier with say ten or eleven. This is not quite as crazy as it sounds, in fact it has been used as a means of scoring a pushover try near the opponent's goal line. Again, on your own put-in, it should be well worthy of further experiment.

Another major source of primary possession is the line-out which has unlimited room for development provided one skill is mastered; that skill is throwing-in. People are inclined to disbelieve that a wing may be picked for his throwing-in ability in preference to someone with better handling and running skills. When you remember that there are fifty to sixty line-outs in a match and say each wing has a quarter of them, then it is not as surprising as you think.

Most of the line-outs are still jammed up to the five yard line, and whilst whole-heartedly agreeing that spaces left in the line-out are a source of potential danger to your own scrum half, with an accurate torpedo throw-in the possibilities for line-out variations would increase enormously.

At the moment it is very difficult to move the ball to the blind or short side of the field; there is just not enough room. However, if you move the whole line-out in-field ten, fifteen, or twenty yards depending on the accuracy of the throw-in, you will have two sides to attack and this must add to the scope of the game. If the torpedo throw could become a skill executed as well as kicking, then it could be used more often in loose play for switching the point of attack. How much time is spent on this skill?

Near perfection in the skill of rucking by the New Zealanders has had an enormous influence on their game, as well as that of the Home Unions. To say that New Zealand has had the edge in this phase of the game is to make the understatement of the century and unless we can become that much fitter than they are and as a result make the game much more fluid, then we too will be forced to master this unit skill.

The point to remember about the ruck is that it brings all the opposition forwards to a particular spot and normally engulfs an opposition back at the same time, so that one side has a numerical superiority over the other.

Many sides are now finding that to move the ball to the short or blind side of the field after a ruck is not always paying the dividends that it used to when they first tried it, because the opposition are leaving a forward out to cover this move. Therefore the point made on page 126 is particularly important and half backs must use their eyes to see which side of the field is least guarded.

Although there are usually few short penalty kicks taken in a match, one or two intriguing moves have been developed from them during the last two seasons. Anything that presents the opposition with problems is worthy of consideration and therefore this part of the game should continue to be developed.

The last phase of the game that needs thought is counter-attack. There have been plenty of full backs who have entered the back line as an extra man, but this is not counter-attacking. The latter takes place when the opposition have, for example, misplaced a kick, or if someone has been tackled and the ball is scooped up and immediate progress made to the opposition goal line. I have made no secret about the duty of the full back in this respect, but it is the duty of all players, especially wings and loose forwards, to see this as a normal means of giving the game its aimed-for continuity. There has been an increase quite recently in the amount of deep diagonal kicking to both the open and blind sides of the field.

Naturally this means the full back or wing is having to run into a corner to retrieve the ball and if the opposition wing and outside centre are hard on his heel, then it is difficult to do anything other than put the ball into touch. That is unless the full back or wing has immediate support from the other and at the same time the defending sides, centres and outside half get back smartly to help. If these things happen then it is perfectly possible to counter-attack.

I have mentioned on page 118 how some sides are playing the blind side wing as an extra full back or extra attacker and this serves to illustrate the need for more than one line of support in attack, defence or counter-attack. For example, forwards chasing a kick-off should never find themselves in one flat line, nor should forwards in support of the man with the ball. There must be depth to every attacking, defending or counter-attacking situation.

If we can briefly cast our eyes back to figure 2 on page 31 it should be evident by now that the desired transformation of performance at all playing levels through coaching is an aim well within our scope. Our ATTITUDE must be right; this means that our efforts should be geared towards the team.

Captains and coaches should use the correct terminology,

and coach by exception. No individual ability or flair should be ruined, although it must be educated and disciplined to operate within that team's pattern of play. This pattern should be understood, accepted, drilled and realized on the field of play by every member of the team.

Variety is absolutely essential, but only operating on top of the basic team skills. This, of course, is where self-discipline plays such a vital part. Above all else the aim must be for perfection in everything – for example, a full turn out on a practice night, knowledge of the laws, correct team numbering from left to right, etc.

Next our APPROACH must be the correct one, that is everyone should understand the key factors (4 to 7 inclusive), of Chapter Five. For example, if we want to produce a more fluid and free-flowing game, and this is what I have been advocating throughout this book, not only will the attitudes of players, and forwards in particular, have to undergo a fundamental change, but so will our approach to the game. You do not produce highly skilful and mobile forwards by playing negative, stereotyped rugby – you only produce them by playing a ' running and handling ' game with 15 players taking part and not just the 7 backs that we have tended to rely on over the years.

Consequently the ACTION that we take must be premeditated and not casual or off-the-cuff. This means the coaching programme at all levels must reflect the organizer's deep understanding of the philosophy of the game and show how the key factors for success are implemented.

Once the long-term plan has been drawn up it should show progression in the same way that academic subjects do; it must also take into account that someone in a school or club must be able to coach others in the art of coaching, so that the maximum coverage of the philosophy and key factors does take place. This sort of communication and co-operation will ensure that there is a continuity between and within all the various playing levels of the game.

A negative attitude, an incorrect approach, or no action, are going to work against any transformation of performance, but this need not happen if everyone accepts the challenge that has been laid before them.

There is no time like the present.

Bibliography

RUGBY TEXTBOOKS

A Guide for Coaches – (Rugby Football Union).
A Guide for Players – (Rugby Football Union).
Rugby on Attack – Ron Jarden (Whitcombe & Tombs).
Rugby – Danie Craven (R. Beerman Ltd, Cape Town).
Tactical and Attacking Rugby – Izak van Heerden (Barrie & Jenkins).
Highspeed Rugby – E. S. and W. J. Higham (Heinemann).
Modern Rugby – Gerwyn Williams (Stanley Paul & Co).
Successful Rugby – Donald Ireland (Pelham Books).

RUGBY TOURS

Beaten by the Boks (1960 All Blacks in South Africa) – Terry McLean (A. H. & A. W. Reed of Wellington).
All Blacks Tour 1963-4 – Andrew Mulligan (Souvenir Press).
Bok Busters (1965 Springbok Tour of Australia & N. Zealand) – Terry McLean (A. H. & A. W. Reed of Wellington).
Lion Tamers (1966 Lions Tour) – Terry McLean.
All Black Magic (1967 All Blacks Tour) – Terry McLean.
All Blacks 1967 – David Frost (Whitcombe & Tombs).
The 1968 Lions (in South Africa) – John Reason (Eyre & Spottiswoode).
On Trek Again (Lions in South Africa 1968) – J. B. G. Thomas (Pelham Books).
Springbok Invasion (1969-70 Tour) – J. B. G. Thomas (Pelham Books).

RUGBY HISTORIES

Illustrated Centenary History of the Rugby Football Union (R.F.U.).
History of New Zealand Rugby Football – Vol 1 (1870-1945) – Swan and Heston (Whitcombe & Tombs).

Haka! The All Blacks Story – Winston McCarthy (Cassell).
The Lions – Wallace Reyburn (Stanley Paul).
World of Rugby – Wallace Reyburn (Elek Books Ltd).

RUGBY – MISCELLANEOUS

Rugby Companion – Wallace Reyburn.
Great Contemporary Players – J. B. G. Thomas (Stanley Paul).
Men, Matches and Moments – J. B. G. Thomas (Pelham Books).
Playfair Rugby Football Annual – (Dickens Press).
Black, Black, Black – Morrie MacKenzie (Minerva Ltd, Auckland).
Fifty-two Famous Tries – J. B. G. Thomas (Pelham Books).
Rugby in Black and Red – J. B. G. Thomas (Pelham Books).
Rugby – Success Starts Here – D. Robinson (Michael Joseph).

PHYSICAL FITNESS

Circuit Training – Morgan and Adamson (Bell & Sons Ltd).
Strength Training for Athletics – R. J. Pickering (A.A.A.).
Bench Weight Training – A. Murray (Kaye).
An Introduction to Tests and Measurement in Physical Education – W. R. Campbell and N. M. Tucker (Bell and Sons Ltd).

Glossary

The following terms and definitions are used in the Rugby Football Union publications for specific use in the coaching field, but they should also be used whenever practicable.

PRACTICE. A session given over to one or more of the following:
  (a) **Training.** A term only to be associated with physical fitness.
  (b) **Teaching.** A term to describe instruction on skills – individual and unit – and thereby the introduction of new techniques.
  (c) **Coaching.** A term for the improvement and development of skills and techniques – unit and team.

INDIVIDUAL SKILLS
  (a) Those individual skills which are basic to all players, e.g., passing, tackling.
  (b) Those which are positional and affect only certain players, e.g., scrum half passing, catching in the line-out, shoving and hooking.

UNIT SKILLS. Skills performed in co-operation with others where the whole team is not involved, e.g., scrum, line-out, flank forwards, No 8 and half backs; threequarter backs and full back.

TEAM SKILLS. Practising the co-ordination of units and involvement of all fifteen players.

QUALITY POSSESSION. Possession by correctly timed feeding of the ball so that positive and constructive play can be achieved from scrum, line-out, ruck, maul, or broken play.

GAIN LINE. The imaginary line drawn across the field through a scrum, line-out, ruck, maul, penalty and kick-offs.

TACKLE LINE. The mid-line betweeen the backs which pivots in relation to the gain line according to the position of the teams, i.e. whether the back divisions are lying shallow or deep.

EFFECTIVE AREA. A part of the field of play, beyond the gain-line, into which the ball is played in such a way that possession can be regained/retained and further attacks developed.

SCANNING. Looking, critically and constructively, at the development around you.

SWITCHING. A term used as a logical follow-on from scanning in that having assessed the situation you change direction of play to avoid the development of dead or negative situation and to cause confusion and disorganization in the defending side.

SCRUM. Refers always to what has been so often called set-scrum.

RUCK. Refers to what has been so often known as ' loose-scrum '. Rucks must be forceful and in no way loose.

MAUL. A situation where players from both sides are gathered round the ball which is not on the ground.

WEDGE. An interlocking, forward formation, usually in a line-out, to ensure quality possession.